Free Spirit

Born to Wander

By: Joei Carlton Hossack

Skeena Press
PMB 9385, P.O. Box 2428
Pensacola, Florida 32513-2428

SkeenaPress@Hotmail.com

September 30, 2005.
To Bob & Janet
We pass this way only once. Enjoy the journey
Joei Carlton Hossack

All rights reserved. No part of this book may be reproduced or transmitted in any form or by any means, electronic or mechanical, including photocopy, recording or any information storage or retrieval system, without written permission from the publisher, except by a reviewer who may quote brief passages.

Published by: Skeena Press
                  PMB 9385, P.O. Box 2428,
                  Pensacola, Florida 32513-2428
                  SkeenaPress@Hotmail.com

Distributed by: Alexander Books
                  65 Macedonia Road,
                  Alexander, North Carolina 28701
                  1-800-472-0438
                  www.aBooks.com

Copyright: Joei Carlton Hossack 2004

Edited: Joei Carlton Hossack
                  Kathy J. Happle

Cover Design: Brion Sausser
                  www.BookCoverDesigner.com

ISBN Number: 0-9657509-5-7

Library of Congress Control Number: 2004090852

Printed in USA
Printing 10 9 8 7 6 5 4 3 2

By the Same Author

Restless From the Start
Everyone's Dream Everyone's Nightmare
Kiss This Florida, I'm Outta Here
A Million Miles from Home
Alaska Bound and Gagged

Available from

aBooks Distributing
65 Macedonia Road,
Alexander, North Carolina 28701

www.aBooks.com
1-800-472-0438

Awards:

Do We Ever Change?
Honorable Mention, Port Aransas Writing Contest

The Agony of De-Feet
A Fine Bit of Madness
Reprinted from the 2004 Benjamin Franklin award-winning
RV Traveling Tales: Women's Journeys on the Open Road
Edited by: Jaimie Hall and Alice Zyetz

RV Traveling Tales: Women's Journeys on the Open
Road may be ordered at:
www.rvtravelingtales.com

For Paul and David

Their *Free Spirit* and lust for life brought joy and happiness to all they touched.

Free Spirit

1. The Piece of Paper
2. The Bird's Nest

Born to Wander

The Piece of Paper

"Where's Harry?" asked my mother as she walked to the door, opened it and looked out onto the street and sidewalk in both directions.

"I dunno," I responded. "I came here by myself."

"How did you get here?" she asked, not looking terribly concerned or upset.

"I took two buses," I told her, taking a deep breath and puffing out my chest, rather proud of myself.

She ignored me and went back to work for a few minutes before asking again, "Where's Harry?"

"I dunno," I answered again. "He didn't come home so I asked Mrs. Greer how to get here on the bus," I said handing my mother the neatly folded piece of paper with the directions on it.

I was five years old in the late forties. There wasn't a label for my situation at that time because so few women worked outside of the home. Today I would be called a "latchkey" kid.

My Rumanian-born father worked at the fruit and vegetable terminal and auction. He left the house six days a week in the middle of the night, around four in the morning, and returned from work around noon, after all the stores had purchased their fresh produce for the day. In addition to this full-time job, he operated his own grocery store for a short while.

I cannot ever remember my short, round, red-haired mother not working. Most of the time she worked in a factory. She did the intricate beading on hats. That was her day job.

Joei Carlton Hossack

When that job was over for the day she worked in my father's store, not coming home until late at night.

My oldest brother, Nathan, was seventeen at the time. He ignored me most of the time. Harry, two years younger than Nathan, was my favorite. He was usually my baby-sitter, my protector, my idol and the wildest fifteen-year-old on Champagneur Street in the Outremont district of Montreal. Harry was the person I looked to for ideas and usually wound up in some kind of trouble for it. My sister, Mona, and I fought constantly. Even though she was five years older than I was, she felt it was her job in life to torment me. She performed her job admirably.

Harry was supposed to be around, staying some place close to the house. I couldn't find him. Perhaps I never even looked. I asked a neighbor, Mrs. Greer, where my parents' store was located. Since Mrs. Greer often prepared lunch for me during school days, a necessity paid for by my mother, and occasionally took care of me after school when my parents were going to be especially late, this information was kept handy and available at her fingertips. On this particular day, for the first time, I asked for directions.

I don't think that Mrs.Greer would have assumed that I would use those directions to go traipsing around the city looking for the store and my mother. But I did. I followed them exactly. I walked to the corner of the next street and waited for and got on the correct bus. Since the directions were written out, the bus driver assumed I was permitted to do this and told me where to change buses and what number to look for in the bus window. After getting off the second bus, again thanks to the directions that were neatly written out, the bus driver took my hand as we crossed busy St. Lawrence Boulevard complete with streetcar tracks down the center. He pointed me in the right direction. I walked the half block to

Free Spirit

Fred's Fruit and Vegetable Market. I walked into the store so proud of myself.

That piece of paper might have been the start of my mother's heart problems. I know that it was the beginning of my free spirit and love of adventure. I was Born to Wander.

The Bird's Nest

I prayed all the time and with all my might, hoping that He would listen. "Please don't give me red, kinky hair like my mother," I said silently every time I saw her trying to fix her hair in any way, shape or form. I was not aware at that time or for years to come that it should have been two separate prayers i.e. please don't give me red hair. Please don't give me kinky hair.

I don't remember exactly when I lost my nickname. As a child my oldest brother Nathan always referred to me simply as "The Bird's Nest" and at the time I could not have imagined why.

Even as a toddler life presented more than its share of challenges. The thought of my mother coming at me with a comb sent me cowering in terror. The hairbrushes in the 1940's did nothing but skim the surface and a comb was needed to take out the tangles. When my mother lost patience, I ended up in tears.

In the 1960's, hair was worn long and straight. I did the best I could to accommodate. My hair hung to the middle of my back, worn most of the time in two ponytails. Occasionally I took the time to braid it. When it hung loose, the smallest amount of humidity in the air produced the largest scouring pad in existence.

Recently my niece confided that her earliest remembrance of me was laying my head on the ironing board and trying to remove the kinks from my hair with a hot iron. Those were the old days and certainly not the good ones where my tresses were concerned.

Free Spirit

By the 1980's, my hair was salt-and-pepper gray and cropped short. Besides cutting it four times a year, I washed it, towel dried it and more often than not, I comb my hair with my fingers. If anyone asked "who does your hair?" I just smiled.

It took fifty years, but I finally appreciate having started life as "The Bird's Nest."

1. Do We Ever Change
2. The Age of Innocence
3. Does This Product Have A "Best If Used Before" Date
4. The Accident   Part 1
                           Part 2
                           Part 3
                           Part 4

The Wild Years

Do We Ever Change?

When Abraham was told by his God to sacrifice his son Isaac we know one thing for sure. Isaac was not a teenager at the time. Had he been a teenager, it would not have been called a sacrifice, it would have been called justifiable homicide. I was that kind of teenager.

I won't describe the fist fights I got into or the foul language I used in school. I won't go into how I used to ditch school in favor of an afternoon movie or how I smoked or always threatened to run away from home; however, only I could get away with such nonsense.

(A) Being the baby of the family was definitely in my favor.

(B) My parents spoiled me rotten.

(C) I could pull a migraine headache out of thin air so whatever I did I was never reprimanded. "Don't yell. She'll get sick" was always on my mother's lips.

The incident that springs vividly to mind occurred when I was fifteen years old. I had an exceptionally smart mouth at the time, as did every other teenager, and at five feet nine inches I towered over the mother.

Much to the relief of my parents I had spent six weeks during that summer visiting my sister who was living in California. I experienced my first taste of real freedom. While Mona worked all day I had the run of her apartment. When her future husband, Marv, needed a rest from the rigors of law school he picked me up and took me to the beach for a couple of hours. Otherwise I had the days to myself. I met everyone living in the two-story apartment building on Sepulveda Boulevard at the swimming pool, something only dreamed

Free Spirit

about at my home in Montreal, Canada and had experienced my first major crush on a twenty-two year old blond hunk named Bruce.

My parents arrived during the last week of my vacation. We were all going to attend the wedding of my sister and her fiancé and on the day after the wedding, my parents and I would be going back to Canada. At that time Mona and Marv could embark on married life and leave on a short honeymoon.

That's when the problems started. My parents wanted to book our return flight to Canada and I calmly announced that I would sooner be caught dead then fly home with them.

"I'm taking a bus," I said coolly.

"You're flying home with us," my mother insisted.

"I'm not a baby. You don't have to hold my hand anymore, you know," I argued. "I got here by myself. I can get home by myself."

"You're coming home with us," she said, her face turning red with anger.

"I'm not going," I retorted.

Her shoulders hunched in resignation. There was a pleading look at my father. "Say something to her, Fred," my mother begged.

To make a short story even shorter, after the wedding and just before they flew home, my parents delivered me to the Greyhound Bus Terminal in downtown Los Angeles. Another "win" for the mouth, for what they would describe to their friends back home as a grueling four-day, three-night trip through hell.

For me, this was heaven. I sat staring out the window feeling a deep-down ache of sadness. My newfound freedom was coming to an end all too soon. I watched as the scenery changed from the hustle and bustle of the big city to a few scattered farmhouses of the country to the wide-open spaces.

Joei Carlton Hossack

I sat on the bus but my spirit was in the saddle with the men I saw in the distance on horseback. The people I spoke with were from different parts of America and since none were traveling as far as I was, there was always someone new sitting beside me. It was thrilling being on my own and the following morning after a very restless night's sleep, I loved walking around the western town of Rock Springs, Wyoming.

My love affair ended abruptly. I returned to discover that I had been walking too long and the bus had left without me. My luggage remained secure in the belly of the bus and some hand luggage had been left in the overhead rack above seat number twenty-eight.

"Everyone was out looking for you. Where did you go?" asked the older waitress looking very concerned.

"Just walking around the town," I answered, trying desperately to gain control of my lower lip that had started quivering.

Horrified at my current predicament, I sat down to have a cup of coffee. Wild thoughts started creeping into my mind. *I can't wait at the restaurant until the next bus. God knows when it'll arrive. Where was my luggage and how was I going to get it back? I can't stay in a motel. I'm only fifteen years old. I have enough money for food and junk, not for a motel. Oh my God. What would Harry do in this situation?*

What would Harry do in this situation was my first rational thought. He is my brother and he was forever getting me into trouble like I couldn't do it well enough on my own. He is also ten years older than I am. The thought came to me in a flash. "Hitchhike, of course!"

With the help of the waitress who called the Greyhound head office, I learned that the next bus stop was two hundred and sixty miles east in Cheyenne, Wyoming. I called the dispatcher at the bus depot in Cheyenne and asked if someone

Free Spirit

could take all my luggage, including what I had stowed over seat number twenty-eight, off the bus and "I'll get there as soon as I can."

They had already received word that a passenger had been left behind in Rock Springs. The Greyhound dispatcher knowing that I was a young girl did not dare ask how I was going to get there "as soon as I can." He just promised to have my luggage waiting.

The year was 1959 and the highways and byways of middle America were a lot safer. Although I looked much older, a woman was considered less of a threat, so I expected I wouldn't have any trouble getting a ride. Since the car that stopped for me had a couple of youngsters in it, perhaps the parents recognized my long thin legs and lanky body as that of a teenager despite my height. Their children were only a few years younger than I was.

The thrill of hitchhiking was over. The two hundred and sixty-mile trip was totally uneventful. We played word games and "I spy" in the back seat. Mr. and Mrs. Wilder treated me to a burger and fries lunch a few hours later and when we approached Cheyenne they asked if I would like to continue with them to Rome, New York.

I thanked them and declined their kind offer. Being with them would have been the same as being with my parents. That was definitely not for me.

In the bus depot my luggage was waiting in a small heap at a desk behind the counter. The stationmaster rerouted my ticket. I was put on another bus almost immediately and told to save my wanderings until I got home.

No one would be the wiser unless I told the story.....and I told the story to everyone, including my horrified parents.

The rest of the "ordeal" as my parents liked to call it was a breeze and memories of that trip, my first trip, remain one of

Joei Carlton Hossack

the highlights of my early days. If my parents were alive today they would be in a constant state of shock over my escapades.

I have remained the same. I still take long bus rides. I still miss flights, buses and trains. I still love talking to strangers. I am still intrigued by new places and, my friends tell me, that I still have the same smart mouth.

In my mind I am still that fifteen-year-old girl.

The Age of Innocence

I was at the age when the only reason I would go along with my parents was if they were going someplace I really, really, really wanted to go and only if I could bring a friend along to relieve the hours of boredom getting there. That was how Arlene, my classmate from Baron Byng High School and I got to go from boring Montreal to exciting Plattsburgh, New York.

I was fourteen years old, very tall and thin with long, spindly legs like those of a newborn colt. My hair was shoulder length, woody brown and kinky-curly to the point of having a mind of its own. When it was hot and humid my hair became a gigantic scouring pad.

Arlene was thirteen years old and reasonably well-developed for her age. She stood an inch or two above five feet while I towered over her at five feet nine inches. Her hair was dark, shiny brown and straight with wispy bangs. Standing side by side, we looked like Mutt and Jeff.

It was late morning when we arrived at the motel where my cousin Mitzi, her husband Jacob and daughter Ruth, who was a couple of years younger than I was, were spending their week of holidays. My parents unloaded from their car, a huge basket of fruit and a small suitcase with our bathing suits, caps and towels. They were preparing for an afternoon of lounging around the pool when I notified them that Arlene and I were going for a walk and would be back in a few hours.

That wasn't what they were expecting but they didn't argue since I was fourteen going on twenty-five. Arlene was willing to go anywhere I wanted as long as there was adventure involved. It was a gorgeous day and my family didn't need me around to spoil it for them by whining and being a typical sullen teenager. They tried to insist that we take Ruth along with us but fortunately she preferred to spend her time at the pool and in the water.

We walked along the main road until we were out of sight of the motel. I grinned at Arlene. She grinned back at me. We stuck our thumbs out as if on cue and were picked up almost immediately by two young Airmen in uniform.

"Where ya heading, girls?" asked Jim, the cute blond one sitting in the passenger seat of the Chevy convertible.

"We're just doing a little sightseeing," answered Arlene. "Can you take us to where all the stores are?"

"Want to see where we live and work?" asked Bobby. "Let's go for a coke at the commissary."

Arlene and I couldn't believe our luck. "Yea, let's go," we said almost in unison.

We rode through the gates with our escorts almost like we owned the place. They waved at the guards on duty who never asked who we were, where we were going or what we planned on doing. Obviously this was something the guys did all the time and in broad daylight no one seemed to worry.

We drove around the base, looking at all the drab-looking buildings and wondered silently what rows and rows and rows of beds looked like with trunks at the foot of each and without the slightest bit of privacy, as Jim described it.

We walked into the commissary and found a table near the jukebox while Jim brought back cokes for all of us. We didn't last long. They had to get back to work. We thanked them before they took us back to the main street and let us out. We walked about a block to a busy intersection where there was a cop directing traffic.

"No hitchhiking here, young ladies," he said.

Free Spirit

"You'd better turn around then because we have to get back to the motel and that's the only way we can get there," I said.

The minute the cop went back to directing traffic a guy picked us up in a mint green convertible with the top down. We waved as we drove off. The policeman waved back.

"Hey," said the big, tall, blond hunk behind the wheel as he pulled away from the curb, "how old are you anyway?"

Arlene immediately responded with "I'm eighteen" and I told the truth. "I'm fourteen," I said.

The look on his face and the smirk that went with it told the whole story. He didn't believe either one of us. He introduced himself as Courtland Wood and after showing us some of the sights of his fair town, he drove us back to the motel and let us off right in front. He was almost too cute for words and I didn't want to get out of the car. He was six-foot-four inches tall, (and I believed him when he told us) had big, broad shoulders like those of a football player and blond hair cut in a brush cut.

I could see my mother standing beside the pool looking my way. With the look on her face I knew I was in trouble.

It was a time of innocence. We enjoyed that time and tried to relive some of it when we got back to Montreal. Arlene and I used to hitchhike all around the city until some guy took us to a deserted park and expected more than we were willing to give, which boiled down to pleasant but sarcastic conversation. Scared out of our wits, we jumped out of the car. We ran as fast as we could back to the main street that circled the perimeter of Beaver Lake looking over our shoulders every few minutes. We had no choice. We hitchhiked home, relieved to get out of the park safely.

The age of innocence didn't last long. We never hitchhiked together again.

The wonderful thing about a "Date from Hell" is that it doesn't matter how many years go by, that "Date" remains fresh in your mind like it happened yesterday. This story took place back in the 1960's.

Does This Product Have a "Best If Used Before" Date?

"No, I'm sorry. I don't understand. Brian told you I was a bitch and the worst date he's ever had and you wanted to see for yourself?" I said, my voice taking on an incredulous tone. "Are men really from this planet?" I thought.

When I would return to Montreal, Canada from my newly adopted home in Los Angeles, California, there would be a flurry of activity from my friends and family. Who could introduce me to "that special someone" so I would change my plans and stay in Canada? To that end nobody ever came close, however, I usually enjoyed the string of dates that were arranged for me. The guys were always eager to meet a "California Girl" even if I did work in an office and had no plans on going into "show biz."

At the ripe old age of eighteen I had left my home in Montreal and was now in my early twenties. I was tall, slender and dark-haired with a natural streak of gray at the front. I had developed a quick wit and a very sharp tongue during the years of fending for myself. I could banter with the best of them.

"Hello Joei. This is Marc, a friend of Rena's," a pleasant, deep sounding voice wafted through the telephone wires.

Free Spirit

"Oh, hi," I replied. "Any friend of Rena's is a friend of mine. Haven't seen her this week. What's she doing?" I asked. "The usual," came the reply. "She's rehearsing for a play."

Rena, a classmate from my high school days, should have been the California girl, I thought. She had the face of a porcelain doll with large doe-like brown eyes, full lips that curled into a pout and skin that was pale and flawless without a hint of makeup. Her dark hair cascaded around her shoulders in soft curls. Even by Hollywood standards, she was a beauty.

"Rena said that you'll be here just a few more days. Want to grab a bite to eat and go to a show tonight?" he asked.

"I'd love to," I answered. "What time?"

"How about six?" Marc replied getting my address and directions before hanging up the phone.

I was pleasantly surprised when I opened the door. He was noticeably taller than I was. That in itself would have made the date a success since at five feet nine inches I towered over most of my friends and their beaux. He was rather good-looking, even though he was dark-haired while I preferred blond. He seemed to have an easygoing and pleasant manner to add to his other qualities. Even before he opened the car door for me we were already conversing.

"Nice car," I commented, "what year?"

"1963," Marc replied. "It gets me where I want to go."

"And where do you want to go?" I asked.

"How about Schwartz's for smoked meat and then Where The Boys Are?" he responded.

"Rena must have told you that the smoked meat in L.A. is awful. That sounds great," I responded enthusiastically.

Dinner was delightful and we had no trouble making conversation all through our meal. The movie was mediocre

19

but the coffee and dessert afterwards, at one of my pre-Los Angeles hangouts, on Crescent Street, was most enjoyable.

* * * * *

"Now what the hell are you talking about?" I asked sitting in his car in front of the apartment building where my parents lived. "I don't understand how Brian got into our conversation. Brian," I asked mystified, "the jerk I went out with last week? He's a friend of yours? The guy's a moron," I said, my voice becoming a little shrill with sentences starting to run together.

"Brian told me you were the worst bitch he had ever met. I told him I wanted to see for myself how bad you were…..but," said Marc, "I had a terrific time. What happened with Brian?" he asked.

"He's got a new job," I replied, most annoyed at being reminded. "He's in sales now. He spent the entire evening trying to sell me one of his new products…..a cemetery plot. I told him that since I had no intention of living here, I sure as hell wasn't going to die here. When he pulled into our driveway I said goodnight and slammed the door. That was the last conversation I had with your friend…..Mr. Hotshot Salesman."

Marc put his arms around me and squeezed me every so slightly. He shook his head in disbelief. "Oh Christ," said Marc, suddenly trying to control his laughter. "This was fun. Thanks. Have a safe trip back to California."

𝒯he 𝒜ccident

Part 1

I remember the scream. It was one high-pitched screech that stopped everyone within earshot dead in their tracks. I slumped to the ground moaning, lying motionless for a few moments, as the group gathered around.

"Are you okay, boy?" asked the large man standing over me wearing brightly colored cross-country ski garb. "Boy," he repeated louder, "are you okay?"

As Paul knelt down beside me, I cried softly in his ear, "Tell him I'm not a boy."

* * * * *

The start of the day had been perfect for a January twentieth. The sun was shining. The day was crisp, cold and bright enough to require us using sunglasses. It had snowed during the week and although the streets and sidewalks had been shoveled, salted and were free and clear, there was lots of snow heaped in piles on lawns just outside our Green Avenue apartment in downtown Montreal.

We had relaxed over our special weekend breakfast of a cheese omelet with bacon and sautéed mushrooms, toast and a couple of cups of coffee, and I was anxious to get back to reading my book. Paul did the dishes while I curled up on my old couch that over the years had conformed perfectly to my body. I opened the book where I had dog-eared the corner. I instantly picked up the plot where I had left it off. I was just past the middle and the story was getting so exciting that I hated to put it down, but the dishes had been washed, dried and put away and Paul was nagging me. My six-foot-four-inch blond, bespectacled significant other, a term we now use since we were not married at the time, wanted to do anything to get out of the house for the day.

"Let's go cross-country skiing," he begged.

"I'm not in the mood," I confessed. "I really want to finish this book."

"Oh, come on," he moaned, pushing his lower lip out in the pout that I loved. He only did that when he really wanted his own way. He knelt down beside me and puckered up his lips making little kissing sounds but never getting close enough for me to really feel them. "Oh, come on," he whimpered.

"Oh, hell," I said, "okay, let me just finish the chapter."

"Let's go now," he said, puckering up and sending kisses through the air in my direction.

I dog-eared the page and closed the book having read exactly one page.

We dressed quickly, retrieved our cross-country skis from our basement locker and were out the door within a half-hour. We strapped the skis onto the rack on top of Paul's white Mazda. Within a couple of hours we were skiing at Mont St. Hilaire.

Once out in the fresh air, I actually enjoyed the exercise. I preferred staying on the flat working up a sweat while Paul always looked for the thrill of a hill or two and the higher the better. I followed closely in his tracks and when I got nervous on a downhill run, I would hunker down as close to the ground as possible so I wouldn't have far to fall if I found myself going too fast.

We had actually worked our way up almost to the top of the mountain when the accident happened. We were now skiing in a small group of skiers, none of whom we knew. The big guy was first and I watched as he skied to the crest of a slope and disappeared over the edge. A few people in the group

Free Spirit

followed. Paul was next and I followed him. I remember going over the edge…..and that is all I remember.

I had skied too wide and was off the track when the accident occurred. My skis might have hit a root or a rock or they may have crossed under the deep powder snow. I let out one scream and the rest is a bit of a blur.

"Are you okay, boy?" asked the large man standing over me. "Boy," he repeated, are you okay?"

"Can you get up?" asked Paul who was on his hands and knees beside me.

"I think so," I said.

"Come, I'll help you," said Paul.

I couldn't get up. With Paul on one side and the large man on the other, they lifted me to a standing position. With help I managed to get to the top of the hill. When I put any weight on my right leg it slipped out to the side. I sat down on a rock and waited. I looked out into the distance and watched as the large trees covered with snow faded into the background, filling in with a shadowy gray mist. I shook my head, refocused and the trees became large again.

I couldn't be hurt too badly, I thought, since I felt no pain whatsoever. I lost track of time as people, mostly strangers, started milling around.

I don't know who organized the volunteers or who went down the mountain to get help. Suddenly a crew appeared with a toboggan, blankets and ropes. My legs and much of my body were wrapped up snugly, put on the toboggan and tied in. With two skiers at the front, two at the back and one at each side, my gloved hands held onto a ski pole at each side that was offered by rescuers. They skied down the mountain while I glided along.

While Paul left to get the car, I was given a chocolate bar to calm me down or perhaps give me some energy.

Joei Carlton Hossack

It was during the ride to the hospital that Paul knew I was not okay. The heat was blasting out on high and although I knew that I should be warm, I was shaking violently. We arrived at the emergency room. Paul helped me into a wheelchair, pushed me into the waiting room and went to park his car. The emergency room was packed. The other patients insisted that I be seen next. I was trembling so violently, they were afraid that I would fall out of the wheelchair. I was ushered in to get my X-rays before Paul returned.

Everything was happening too fast. By the time the X-rays were taken a doctor in a black overcoat, top hat and white silk scarf was standing at my side. We went into the adjoining room and Paul was asked to come in while we looked at the X-rays. The doctor pointed to each injury in turn. The bone in my right leg was broken an inch below the knee. One ligament was torn and two more were shredded. The cartilage on both sides of the knee was torn. In short, only the flesh and one ligament held the top of my leg to the bottom of my leg.

"We'll have to wait a little while before we operate" said Dr. Helmy. "They should not have given you the chocolate bar. We'll have to wait until it has been digested."

"No," I said, "you can't operate tonight. Let me go home and I'll come back tomorrow. I promise. I'll come back tomorrow," I kept repeating, my voice choking back the tears. "Please let me go home."

"Paul can stay with you until we are ready to operate," the doctor said. "I'm sorry," he said, "you can't go home like this."

Paul left around nine. He kissed me goodnight just as the nurse arrived with shaving equipment. I was wheeled into the operating room an hour later.

The Accident

Part 2

It was in the middle of the night when I awoke. The room was warm with only one dim bulb to light the way. "Where am I?" I asked the nurse standing beside my bed.
"You're in the Recovery Room," she answered softly.
"Can I have some water?" I asked.
"I can give you just a sip," she said. "You're dry from the anesthetic and we don't want you to get sick."
"Do I have a cast on?" I asked as my hand ran down the right side of my body and felt the hard, cold plaster.
It didn't take the rest of the nursing staff long to realize that I was awake, alert and ready to return to my room. "Just press this button if you need something," the nurse said as she handed me a cord with a button on the end of it. She tied it to the end of my bed where I could easily reach it should it become necessary. She left and before closing the door reminded me again to call if I needed anything.
The days in the hospital were long and boring. I had few visitors since almost everyone I knew worked. My father arrived in the early afternoon after he got off work and usually stayed a few minutes, which broke up my day somewhat. I slept a good deal of the time. I watched television the rest of the time. I tried reading and doing needlepoint but my eyes would not focus for more than a few minutes at a time.
By the fourth day I was chomping at the bit. A couple of nurses arrived early in the afternoon with a pair of crutches and I was told that when I could maneuver on the stairs I could go home. I got out of bed. I put the crutches under my arms

Joei Carlton Hossack

and started to take a step. Fortunately the nurses were there to catch me. The cast weighed nine pounds, went from my toes to my hip, and I couldn't move it.

"There's a trick to this," said one of the nurses. "Firstly you must bring up your toes. Your toes must carry the weight of the cast and lift your right hip slightly," she went on.

Within minutes I had mastered it and for the first time made my way into the bathroom alone. By the time I returned I was dripping in sweat and barely made my way back to bed. Within an hour I was at it again. This time I managed to make it down the hall and back and by the time the evening shift arrived I wanted to be taken over to the stairs to practice.

The next day Paul picked me up at noon and delivered me back to our apartment. He settled me on the couch with a bunch of pillows and a blanket and flipped on our new colored television set with remote control that he had purchased while I was in the hospital. He went back to work.

Why the hell was I so anxious to get home! It was Thursday. I was exhausted from the accident, the surgery and the anesthetic, and now I was home alone with no one to even make me a cup of coffee. The kitchen was a marathon away from the living room.

It was around two in the afternoon when my father walked in with the three large avocados that I had begged for. "Oh, thanks Pa," I said and promptly fell asleep for a few minutes. He went into the kitchen and brewed us each a cup of coffee. He washed, dried and put away the breakfast dishes and came back to keep me company. He stayed only long enough to finish the coffee, wash out the mugs and put them away. Monday through Friday at two I became his responsibility for as long as I needed him. We occasionally played cards but he was a shark at gin rummy and his sympathy never ran deep enough to let me win.

Free Spirit

By the next weekend I was feeling well enough to go out for a drive. We spent Saturday night at Paul's sister house in Dollard des Ormeaux, just outside Montreal.

Let me see. How do I explain my lunacy? The week of inactivity had been torture. The wine had loosened up my stiff limbs. The music was exciting. In a few short words I was feeling no pain. Cast and all, I got up and danced the twist no less, supported by the crutches. I loved it. The evening flew by.

The next day, Sunday, I was a bit stiff and sore and by Monday the pain was excruciating. I was hoping that someone would shoot me and put me out of my misery.

I called Dr. Helmy's office early Monday morning and asked to speak to the doctor.

"Who's calling?" asked the receptionist.

"My name is Joei Carlton. Dr. Helmy opera........"

"Oh my dear, we have all heard about you. The doctor is in with a patient. I'll have him call you back the instant he is free. Are you okay?" she asked.

With a sympathetic ear on the other end of the phone line, I immediately broke down into tears. "No," I answered.

The call came within ten minutes. I explained the pain I was in, never telling him why, and he asked if someone could take me over to the hospital. He said he would meet me at the hospital at around five or five thirty. I called Paul at work. He would leave a little early and drive me over.

The hospital was less than a block away but I could not manage it on my own. Paul helped me down the stairs and into the car and helped me out at the other end. We waited for Dr. Helmy.

Upon his arrival, we were ushered into a room the size of a closet. I didn't have to explain much to the doctor. Nor did I tell him that we had been out dancing. I don't think he would

27

Joei Carlton Hossack

have believed me anyway. All he saw was that the cast was too big around my thigh and although I had no feeling in the knee area, it had been hitting against the inside of the cast. It needed to be tighter.

"Do you mind if Paul stays in the room and helps me?" asked Dr. Helmy.

I never even had a chance to answer before the door opened and the janitor walked in and removed a mop. As the buzz saw came down and started to cut from the toe, a nurse entered, walked to the back of the room and removed something from the cabinet. Before the entire procedure was over there must have been a dozen or more people walk in and out of the room, never giving me a second glance even though I was sitting there in my panties.....and the doctor had actually asked if I minded if the person I was living with stayed in the room to help. Paul's job was to assist in pulling apart the thick pieces of plaster that had once been my total protection from the outside world.

I was horrified to see my leg. The eighteen-inch S-shaped scar that ran down the inside of my knee looked like something out of a Frankenstein movie. From the knee down, two weeks of dark stubble now dotted my leg and tiny infections had developed all down my shin where the nurse had nicked it while shaving. What wasn't dark, hairy or infected, was dry and scaly.

Above the knee was another horror. The thigh muscle had atrophied and the flesh hung down leaving an outline of the bone. When I lifted my leg all I saw was the bone. I wanted to be sick. I just knew that I would never walk properly again.

The Accident

Part 3

The cast stayed on for six weeks and although I could give you a day-by-day, blow-by-blow description of life as a cast member, I will spare you the torture. I will tell you only about the highlights of being, what I hoped would be, temporarily crippled.

It was somewhere around the fifteenth of February when I stood at the sink washing the dishes. I had just celebrated my birthday a few days before and physically was feeling a little stronger. The dishes were stacked to one side and the sink was full of hot water and suds. My elbows rested on the front of the sink as I soaked one plate, scrubbed and rinsed it and put it into the other sink.

When Paul approached I half expected him to pick up a dishtowel and start drying. He didn't. He put his hand down the back of my jeans and squeezed my cheek. Had his touch been a gentle one I might have been pleased. Had it been with a caress I would have understood. But it wasn't. He just put his hand down the back of my jeans and squeezed.

"Hey, get your hand out of there," I yelped. "What do you think you are doing?" I asked.

"You're thirty years old now, you know. I'm checking for sag," he said.

"Get your hand out of there. There's no sag," I said.

"Oh yes there is," he said.

"There is not. Get out of there," I said, not enjoying his sense of humor at that moment.

"Oh my God," he said, "you don't know. Do you?"

Joei Carlton Hossack

I swiveled around and glared at him. The smile was gone. He put his arms around me and held onto me, pulling me closer to his chest.

I backed away. "What don't I know?" I asked.

"You know that thigh muscle that had atrophied, well it extends all the way up to your bum," he said. "One cheek sags."

I dried my hands and put my right hand down the back of my jeans. I was devastated. The nightmare just kept getting worse. He held me while I cried.

It was a week or so after that incident when we were invited to an outdoor party. This time we headed up north to the Laurentian Mountains to go ice fishing. The entire day had been planned by several of the men who Paul worked with. Since the year was 1974, you will forgive me if I cannot remember where exactly we went or who everyone was in the party. I do remember a few that were present but there were a dozen or more and only one couple that we socialized with away from work.

We parked our car along with the rest on the banks of the lake. Four small huts had been placed on the ice for us and an auger had been used to drill several holes in the ten-inch thick ice. We took our picnic basket into one of the huts and brought out a couple of deck chairs. Everyone had a picnic basket. Everyone had wine and everyone had beer. We would not go hungry or thirsty on this outing.

Almost everyone had a line in the water, including me. I was handed a glass of wine and so started the festivities. There were a few fish caught but not big enough or numerous enough for anyone to get excited. We fished. We ate. We drank.....a lot. When boredom set in, the men decided to play hockey. Since we were without hockey equipment the game had to be improvised. There were two teams, three on each side. Picnic

Free Spirit

baskets were made into goal posts and I, sitting on a deck chair, was the puck. My leg, still in the cast, was stuck out in front like the lead dog at the Iterod. With a team member hanging on to the back of the chair, I was propelled down the ice towards the goal line. If a block was set up, I was set free and pushed in the general direction to go sliding down the ice on my own and hopefully through the goal posts.

"He shoots. He scores," means far more to me than to most people who don't watch or play or have any interest in hockey.

I don't know how many fish were caught that day but I do know that some of them ended up unwrapped in the trunk of a car whose owner parked his car in a heated garage.

This was one of the best days I remember of being in the cast. We all sobered up at dinner and drove home safely, even though it was a long drive and I was not the only one exhausted from the day's events.

In between the highlights were a lot of long, boring, lonely days and a few equally boring evenings. On one particularly boring evening, I called the wool store to find out if they had, in stock, black Patons and Baldwins needlepoint wool. They did. Although Paul said he would be home in time to drive me over, I chose, out of sheer spite, not to wait. I dressed warmly, stuffed a few dollars into my coat pocket, put the crutches under my arms and away I went. The one and a half block walk to the shopping center took about forty-five minutes. I walked in, dripping in sweat and totally exhausted. I purchased my two skeins of wool, and since the store was just about to close I walked back to the steps and sat down. I cried while I rested, trying to get up the energy for the long walk home. There was no one in the shopping center that I could call for help. The trip back to the apartment took even longer. Paul found me sitting outside on the bottom step of our building. I

Joei Carlton Hossack

couldn't make it up the stairs and there was no one around who could knock on the door for me. I cried and waited until he rescued me.

There were few times in our lives together that I saw him angry. That was one of them.

Less than two weeks later I was at the doctor's office. Before the X-rays were taken, Dr. Helmy advised me that he felt I should be prepared to be in a brace for a few months.

Once I was out of the cast, however, he changed his mind. The knee was as solid as a rock. And I do mean "solid as a rock." It would not bend. It would not straighten. It would not bear weight.

I needed physiotherapy.

The Accident

Part 4

My first days out of the cast were terrifying. To start with, the leg was cold and thin and the thigh muscle hung down like a balloon that had been partially filled with water. The hairs on it were dark, prickly sharp and long enough to braid. The skin felt like sandpaper and no amount of cream was enough to soften it. I was not permitted to walk on my leg for about four more weeks. I was afraid to go outdoors for fear of falling.

It was within a few days when I decided that I didn't need the crutches to walk around the apartment. There was a certain freedom associated with dragging myself from the living room into the kitchen or bedroom and back without benefit of those dreaded sticks even though my underarms and the palms of my hands no longer ached. There was also a certain freedom of being able to sleep with my whole body under the covers. When the cast ended up under the covers my entire leg would swell causing much discomfort and waking me in great pain and panic.

There was that day, however, early in this "freedom stage" when I overdid it even though I had not left the apartment. I had walked around too much. Fatigue had put me to sleep quickly but I awoke soon after in a tremendous amount of pain. I took two of the prescribed painkillers and fell back to sleep almost immediately. I awoke again in pain and assumed that the painkillers had worn off. I took another couple and fell back to sleep. I awoke a third time still in pain. I took more painkillers and fell back to sleep. I awoke again still in pain. I don't know how many hours went by. I didn't know what time it was. All I knew was that it was still dark outside and I was still in a tremendous amount of pain. I decided to take a bath. I ran the water and stepped in while just the bottom quarter of the bathtub was filled. As soon as I sat down the warm water caressed my poor damaged leg. The relief was instantaneous. All six painkillers took effect at once. I sat watching as the warm water filled the tub knowing that I was no longer capable of reaching over and turning off the tap. I sat in a stupor. Had I been alone in the apartment I might have drowned but Paul was in bed sleeping.

The running water became part of his dream but when it didn't stop, it woke him up. He came into the bathroom just as the water was about to overflow the tub. He turned off the tap. He took out the stopper and helped me out of the bathtub. He dried me off, bundled me up in a blanket and I sat on the couch while he made us some coffee. I cried myself to sleep in his arms.

We called the doctor the next morning and discovered that the painkillers, containing codeine, were addictive. I decided never to take another. Paul came home that night with a wide variety of rubs that seemed to have a soothing effect. When I couldn't sleep I would run a bath and sit until the pain went away. I would then get out and try to sleep. If the pain returned, I went into the same bath as long as the water stayed warm.

When physiotherapy started, the pain became excruciating. Every morning at ten, I walked over to the hospital for physiotherapy. I looked upon the weight boot as my friendly mortal enemy. As the muscle was being rebuilt, I gradually lost that one sagging cheek.

It was only when I ran into an intern who was on duty the night I arrived after the accident that I learned how severe

Free Spirit

my injury had been. He was surrounded by a group of interns. When I said, "Hi, do you remember me?" he turned to the others and said, "This is the girl I was telling you about. The one with the......" and rattled off a name with a hundred or more letters. "Hey, we didn't think you would ever walk again. Look at you! What are you doing in the hospital?" he asked.

"I come for physio five times a week. I'm here every morning" I answered.

"You're looking great. Keep up the good work," he said.

It was at the next appointment with Dr. Helmy when I asked why he never told me that he didn't think I would walk again.

"The mind is a very strange thing," he said. "If I told you that you would not walk, you probably never would."

"You've got the wrong girl," I said. "Had you told me that I wouldn't be able to walk, I would have walked in half the time."

Physiotherapy lasted every day for one and a half years. The doctor appointments, every quarter of a year at the end, lasted two years. I started back cross-country skiing while I was still going for physiotherapy. I walk and I bicycle. When I have to stop dancing, please shoot me.

1. *Oh No, A Gray Hair*
2. *Severe Weather Warning*
3. *Lead Me Not…*
4. *Itsy, Bitsy, My Ass*
5. *Wheel of Misfortune*
6. *Hey Buddy, Have You Seen My Wife*
7. *Paws for the Comedienne*

The Married Years

Oh No, A Gray Hair

When does a person go from being prematurely gray.....to gray.

I found my first half dozen strands at the ripe old age of eleven and by twenty years old I had a streak of gray at the front that everyone thought charming.....and phony. One by one they popped up, mostly unnoticed. By age thirty-five the gray hairs were noticed.

I had a flash of brilliance. I made an appointment with a local hairdresser for the following Saturday and couldn't wait for the day to arrive. "Put in gray streaks," I said excitedly.

"Gray?" she asked, the bridge of her nose wrinkling up like I had said something that she didn't understand.

"Gray," I responded.

Three hours later my hair was alive with gray streaks.....some light gray, almost silver, some dark gray like gunmetal, some just plain old grizzled, probably my own natural ones

When my friends and family commented on how gray I had become, "Oh no," came my reply, "I had the hairdresser put in gray streaks. Phony, every last one of them," I grinned. "Makes me look distinguished," I said and I kept saying it month after month after month.

I waited for the walnut brown to return so I could have more gray streaks put in.....but the brown never returned. Horrors, my gray streaks never grew out. Needless to say I never did that again.

So I ask. When does a person go from being prematurely gray.....to gray?

Severe Weather Warning

I sat glued to the television set watching The Arrival (of aliens, no less) with Charlie Sheen, Ron Silver and Lindsey Crouse when the severe weather warning flashed in the corner of the screen.

I looked out the window into the darkness. Wind chimes coming from the cemetery next door indicated that the breeze had picked up a notch and the only streetlight played with my imagination as the weeping willow trees danced to the rhythm in my head. There wasn't even one visible star or a sliver of moon to indicate that I wasn't alone in the universe. I felt agitated and unsettled.

An overnight snowstorm was predicted and I resented it. I would be doing a book signing at the Books-A-Million in the Hoover Plaza, a suburb of Birmingham, Alabama, the next day and I wanted good weather. Although the drive was only about twenty miles, I hated the thought of driving in snow that was possibly going to be mixed with rain. I worried that the customers, unprepared for that kind of inclement weather, would stay home rather than risk disaster.

I fell asleep that night thinking of the wildest and most unusual storm that had ever presented itself to me.

It was on a Friday afternoon, so many years ago, that my husband Paul and I drove out to our fixer-upper farm in Franklin Center, Quebec. By early evening we were nestled under a heavy quilt in front of a glowing fireplace, when the snow started. By the time we were ready for bed there was a foot of snow on the ground. We stayed warm and cozy under an electric blanket. We woke up to flurries and a fifty-foot driveway that would need plowing if we were going to get our car out. We called our neighbor and asked if he could plow us out anytime Sunday morning or early afternoon. He put us on his list.

We puttered around on Saturday after a late start to the day. We shoveled the snow off the balcony and the car. We cross-country skied into the woods behind the house. I started a snowball fight that I had no chance whatsoever of winning before going into the house for a hot toddy, dinner and an evening of reading in front of another roaring fire, one of the joys of country living.

We awoke Sunday morning to a plowed driveway, bright sunshine and a north wind that forced its way through every crevasse and into our old farmhouse. After the usual (getting ready to leave) chores, we laid blankets down across every doorway in the hopes of preserving whatever heat remained in the house.

The howling wind threatened to blow us off course but we drove slowly and steadily down the two-lane roads from Franklin Center towards the Mercier Bridge and our city apartment in Montreal. We were just approaching St. Chrysostome when all traffic came to a dead stop. There were about fifteen cars ahead of us and slowly but surely the backup of cars behind us continued to grow. After twenty minutes we turned off the motor, not knowing the reason for the delay or how long it would be. Gas stations were few and far between on this stretch of road and the fact that it was a Sunday night made it even more intimidating. The wait was over an hour and the car was getting cold. Paul and I bundled up in a Hudson's Bay blanket that we always kept handy so, for the moment, we were okay.

Bright lights heading towards us were the first indication of an active life on the planet. It took us several minutes to realize that a gigantic snowplow was heading our way. What

Free Spirit

followed were fifty or more cars driving at a snail's pace behind the plow. Eventually the plow turned around and took up the lead of the vehicles heading towards Montreal. We headed into a wonderland the likes of which I had never seen before and have not seen since. Blowing snow had drifted across the road and the sides were banked higher than the houses that lined the route. We drove slowly, desperately trying to avert an avalanche that would bury a car or two under heavily compacted snow and ice. Thanks to the plow all the cars made it through safely and we eventually arrived at our Montreal apartment.

    That was my last "severe snowstorm warning." The "severe snowstorm warning" in the Birmingham, Alabama area on December 3, 2000 was to produce possibly as much as an inch. "I'm tough," I said out loud to myself. "I think I can handle that."

    Fortunately it never materialized.

Lead Me Not.....

I was not surprised to see a woman with an old golden retriever, as a seeing eye dog, asking a couple for directions to one of the smaller restaurants. The Scarborough Town Center in North Toronto is such a large shopping plaza that it was easy, even for a sighted person, to become confused. When the couple didn't know where the restaurant was, the blind woman left.

Forty minutes later, after a totally unsuccessful shopping expedition, I passed the restaurant and the woman with the dog was fifty yards ahead of me. I know that she had walked right by the front door and probably not for the first time.

I rushed to catch up to her. "Excuse me. Are you still looking for the restaurant?" I asked.

When she said "yes" I put my arm out and suggested to her that she take it.

"You walked right by the front door," I said. "You are just going to have to teach your dog to read," I commented jokingly.

"He knows exactly where it is. I meet my friends there every couple of days," she said very matter-of-factly. "He's just pissed off because I won't take him for a ride on the escalator."

Itsy, Bitsy, My Ass

Does it seem that whatever we fear the most comes back to haunt us? Is the fact that this is the day before Halloween or is it perhaps because I am now living in the confines of a camper that these eight-legged horrors, which turn my backbone into an icicle dripping one drop of courage at a time, are invading my tiny space? As the weather turns cold I find myself killing a couple each night as they stroll arm-in-arm, arm-in-arm, arm-in-arm and arm-in-arm across my bedroom ceiling mere inches above my face.

It is not the ones I kill that send the shivers down my spine. It is the ones that are left behind to mourn and creep and crawl that I fear. How many are lurking in the closet covered by my favorite sweatshirt or spinning a web under the curtain in my bedroom or eyeing me from above the medicine cabinet in the bathroom waiting to pounce? Each minor encounter reminds me of that night so many years ago.

The year was nineteen eighty. Six of us had boarded a plane. We left behind the ice and snow so prevalent during the month of February in Canada and landed in Paradise.....the Island of Tobago. Our week-long retreat waited. It was a luxury three-bedroom, three-bathroom villa complete with private swimming pool for early morning dips, afternoon lounging and those ever-popular intimate late-night skinny dips. As it happened, each of us, thinking we were sneaking into the pool for a midnight rendezvous to be alone with our lover, were in for a surprise. We laughed when we discovered we all had the same idea.

The maid, who showed up daily before starting her cleaning duties, served a typical island breakfast with lots of fresh fruit that she picked up from a local market on the way. The pool boy came by unannounced each afternoon to clean out the debris and one day a tiny-bodied long-legged spider was scooped up from the depths.

"What is that!" I asked absolutely horrified at the sheer expansiveness of the creature.

"On the Islands here, we call that a spida," he answered.

Okay, I guess I had that one coming.

As long as it was dead I photographed my outstretched hand alongside the arachnid and was repelled when the spindly legs extended well beyond the end of my fingertips. I felt so brave.....and horrified at the same time to think that it once walked the earth or possibly my bedroom and that it probably has oodles of relatives that had not yet been scooped from the bottom of the pool and were still walking the earth or possibly my bedroom with hundreds, possibly thousands, of similar creatures with which I had not as yet come face to face.

Our week in the villa was over all too quickly. Our friends returned to Canada to resume life in the frozen north while Paul and I decided to play another week. Not being able to afford the luxury condo on our own for the next week, we went looking for more modest accommodations. We found a guest house. We were going "native", as Paul liked to call it.

Our room was large with lots of natural rattan furniture, a comfortable bed and an en suite bathroom. That evening we were treated to a fried flying fish dinner complete with rice, lime wedges to squeeze over the top and lots of fresh fruit, a tasty treat we had enjoyed on more than one occasion.

"What's that?" I asked the proprietor/cook/housekeeper, as I pointed to some giant, brown grasshopper-looking insect that had affixed itself to the wall above the doorway.

"It is local," she said. "They do nothing."

Free Spirit

We dropped the matter and went on to discuss other local matters like how long she had lived there, where her children went to school and what they were learning.

It had been a long day. We went to bed early. Paul threw open the shutters and for a brief moment we looked out over the yard and marveled at the banana trees with small green bunches that were just forming.

I don't know what time it was when Paul went into the bathroom but it was still pitch black outside. I was only slightly aware that he had come out of the bathroom and had immediately gone back into it. I was still groggy when he did it again.

"What's the matter?" I asked, wondering if he was feeling all right.

"Just need a towel," he answered, his voice becoming a little high pitched, as he returned to the bathroom for the third time.

He was out again trying to find his shoes in the dark since we had no idea where the light switch was for the bedroom. The light from the bathroom did little to illuminate our room.

"What's going on?" I asked, suddenly alarmed. His answer froze my blood.

"GO BACK TO BED!" he yelled, his voice strangled in a whispered scream as he returned to the bathroom and quickly slammed the door. It was an eternity before he returned.

We turned on all the lights we could find, our fingers fumbling with freestanding lamp switches. We lay in the middle of the bed holding each other until daylight, our eyes darting frantically into every corner and afraid to close them even for a minute and even more afraid of seeing something we didn't want to see. We packed our few belongings, greeted the

Joei Carlton Hossack

owner with the news that we were leaving and ate our breakfast with bloodshot eyes that again darted everywhere.

In the car I asked Paul, who had not as yet told me in so many words, exactly what he had seen. "Was it hairy?" I asked.

"It was huge! It was black! And yes, it was hairy," he answered.

That was our one day of going "native" in Tobago. We checked into a modern hotel with tiny mesh screening on all the windows in our third-floor room, with a swimming pool in the back yard and overlooking the ocean. We enjoyed the rest of our second week in Paradise almost as much as the first.

Yikes, got to go. I think I hear those eight legs scratching at the camper door.

Wheel of Misfortune

I have had one ticket in all my many years of driving. It was for speeding. I was driving forty-three miles per hour in a thirty-five mile zone. Even that ticket might have stemmed from the fact that, upon being shown the radar equipment, I said, "Oh, is that the little gizmo that clocked a tree doing sixty on last Saturday night's news?"

"No Ma'am," said the officer in a humorless, controlled and authoritative voice, as he wrote out the ticket. I have never felt the urge to speed since that day.

I also must confess to six or seven automobile accidents but I have rarely been in the various cars when they were hit. Most of the time the car was parked.....and parked legally, I might add. On the other occasions I had been stopped either at a stop sign, or at a traffic light or in an endless line of stationary traffic, well some of us were stationary before being used as target practice. So why do I know so many people whose driving scares the hell out of me?

My five-foot-tall, red-haired mother did very little of the family driving. She was permitted, by my father, to drive on straight roads, for extremely short periods of time and only when the weather was clear, dry and sunny.....and not too sunny, of course. We were all together on one of those rare occasions when he relinquished the keys to his Pontiac Stratochief to my eager mother. It was on a day-trip from Montreal, Quebec to Plattsburgh, New York when a Highway Patrol officer stopped her. It seemed that she had been driving about ten miles per hour in a fifty mile per hour zone. The officer,

Joei Carlton Hossack

with no respect for age, lacked the sensitivity training so prevalent these days and asked if she had gotten her license in a Cracker Jack box. He then asked that she produce it. That was when she discovered that her sex was listed as "male" on her driver's license. She never drove again.

My father did almost all of the driving and being a passenger in his car could be construed as cruel and unusual punishment, bordering on torture. Being a terrible driver was compounded by the fact that he lacked a sense of direction even in the city that he had lived in most of his life.

The trip that springs to mind, out of the many that I had to choose from, occurred in 1974. That was the year I had a rather debilitating skiing accident. My knee had been pinned and stapled back together so I dared not risk the three hundred and fifty mile drive, by myself, from Montreal to Boston, Massachusetts to attend the wedding of a cousin.

My father, his second wife Celia, and I picked up his niece Mitzi and her husband Jacob. We were off while it was still dark, leaving Mitzi's home around six in the morning. Four hours later and sixty miles away, just over the American border, we stopped for coffee. We had just left the restaurant and were heading towards the car when my father uttered the words that drove me to the brink of insanity.

"And in two hours," he said, "we'll stop for lunch."

"In two hours," I shrieked, "we won't even be in Plattsburgh and that's thirty miles away. How about taking a nap, Pa? I'll drive for awhile," I said through teeth clenched so tightly I felt they were on the verge of splintering.

In one swift motion, he passed me the keys like a runner passes the baton for the next leg of the race. He climbed into the back seat and I limped to the driver's side and parked myself behind the steering wheel. I took a minute or so to

Free Spirit

familiarize myself with the workings of his huge Pontiac. It didn't take good ole boy, Fred, long to fall asleep.

About four hours later he awoke with a jolt. He was very agitated. "I can't sleep when you drive," he said. "Where are we?"

"Just outside of Boston, Pa," I replied.

Needless to say I was recruited to drive the return trip as well.

My husband, Paul, however, was the worst of the bad lot of drivers. He was so sure of himself that he loved to test his reflexes behind the wheel of his car. For every ten miles per hour of speed he felt that an inch or two behind the car in front was sufficient. His tailgating terrified me and, on more than one occasion, we found ourselves on two wheels pulling into another lane so as not to smash ourselves into the car in front of us.

On a humorous note, and there were very few humorous notes while we were commuting to and from work, we picked up my sister from the airport. We drove her to my brother's house. Paul pulled into my brother's driveway. Since Nathan's car was already in the driveway the back end of our car was still on the sidewalk.

My sister, Mona, directed him. "Pull up, Paul." He inched his way closer and closer. "Pull up," said my sister. "Come on, Paul," said Mona, "you drive closer than that to cars on the highway. Pull up." WHACK! "Okay, Paul," said Mona. "That's close enough."

I'm sorry to say that in recent years, I've met some drivers that make Paul's driving seem like a Sunday stroll around the park. Did all of these awful drivers in my life prepare me for the highway and byways in and around Sarasota, Florida where I spent my winters?

It's very scary out there on them roads, my friends.

Hey Buddy, Have You Seen My Wife?

"Same as Paul's on the side, a little longer on top," was my standard answer to Sam when he asked how I wanted my hair cut. Paul, my always impeccably dressed, investment dealer husband, had neatly trimmed blond hair on the sides and nothing on top.

It took one disastrous haircut and a year or more of Sam the Barber, my next door neighbor at my wool shop, asking if he could cut my hair before I trusted him to take a scissors to my unruly mop of kinky curly, salt and pepper, gray hair.

The unfortunate incident occurred on one of my days off. I was particularly looking forward to the day because in the preceding week my hair had grown that fraction of an inch too long on top and had instantly gone wild enough to hide a growing family of wildebeest. I walked around with my fingers constantly combing through my hair trying to keep it under control. It never worked.

I always looked forward to getting it cut. I liked it short, as straight as I could get it and, most importantly, out of my eyes. I gave the hairdresser the abbreviated order "short, please" and let my beautician do her magic. Janie, who worked at a salon close to my Toronto Beach area home, had cut my hair on numerous occasions, so I didn't give it a moment's thought and went back to reading one of the many gossip newspapers that had been scattered about the coffee table.

I took one quick glance while she was cutting the top and when all appeared normal I turned the page to another sordid tale about some actress or other and relaxed. With the next glance my eyes popped out in disbelief. What the hell had she done! The top was shorter than I had ever seen it. Had I

Free Spirit

been a teenage boy it would have been called a brush cut. The one side that she had cut was so short that each individual hair took on a life of its own and stood straight out.

I picked up the brush to see what I could do. I brushed the side backwards and then forwards. No amount of brushing would make it lie flat. I had no other recourse but to have her duplicate the side. My new look was atrocious.

"Oh, what the hell," I said, under my breath, resigning myself to the situation. There was no point in making an all-out scene although I would have been well within my rights. There were no important functions in the near future. No family or business dinners were coming up any time soon and my hair grew really quickly, I thought. I paid the bill. I tipped her less than half what I would have normally and left. I went home, busied myself with other projects and soon forgot about the disastrous haircut.

Paul telephoned around five that afternoon. "I'm glad you're home, Hon," he said. "I locked my keys in the car. If you bring my spare set I'll buy us a really nice dinner."

"A deal," I said. "I'll meet you at King and Bay, southwest corner. I'm leaving in five minutes."

I cursed and swore at the rush hour traffic in downtown Toronto and was relieved when I saw Paul standing on the corner waiting patiently, folding back a page of the newspaper. He opened the passenger side door, looked at me and quipped, "hey buddy, have you seen my wife?"

"Shut up and get in. Let's get out of here," I retorted. Upset with the traffic, I was not prepared for a lengthy discussion about my hair. "Besides," I reminded him, "it's still longer than yours."

"Touché," was his only remark.

The following morning while unlocking the door to my wool shop I poked my head into Sam's Barber Shop. He

Joei Carlton Hossack

looked and pointed. "And you paid for that?" he quipped, hardly able to control his laughter. Three months later Sam cut my hair for the first time.

    That was over ten years ago. In 1989 I closed my wool store to go traveling with my husband. In 1992 my beautiful Paul died of a heart attack and I resumed a rather chaotic, nomadic life, but twice a year Sam still cuts my hair. In October before I leave for Florida and in April before I leave for parts unknown, I stop on the Danforth for a haircut and a talk with my friend.

Paws For The Comedienne

Part 1

Only once in a person's life does a dog like Skeena come along.....hopefully. She was named for the scenic, swift-moving river in British Columbia, Canada. As an adult dog she weighed about eighty-five pounds, had flashing brown eyes that turned demonic as soon as she put her ears back, and a coat so thick that a blanket could have been woven from her hair and undercoat. Her face was that of a wolf but the perfect mask was that of a finely bred champion. She was a gorgeous Alaskan malamute and from day-one she made my life pure hell.

We had prepared a place for her in our kitchen with her own squeaky toys, a comfortable blanket, a hand-painted water bowl and a brightly colored food dish. We were really excited about our new arrival. All the way over we discussed names but in the end decided to wait until a marking or a trait jumped out at us. We picked her up from the breeder, about five miles from our two-story country home on three acres in Beeton, Ontario, on a warm, sunny day in August 1980. She looked like a baby raccoon.

Paul picked her up and held the chubby little ball of fluff at arm's length. In a soft manly voice he said, "Hi little girl" and then cuddled her. She nestled in, licked his face and from that instant I became the enemy. Only I stood between her and the love of her life.

Paul handed me the pup, opened my car door and I sat down with her against my chest. She stood up on her hind legs, her front legs stretching up my body, with her paws resting on my shoulders, and started to cry and howl. We hadn't even left the driveway when that nonsense started. Paul leaned over and

Joei Carlton Hossack

stroked her back. She stopped crying instantly. I held her while Paul drove and stroked her back all the way home.

In time the situation got no better. Skeena became part of the family and from my point of view she was a part of the family we could do without. Needless to say the feelings were mutual. To her, I was nowhere close to the top in the chain of command and thus expendable, except, of course, that it was my job to keep her food and water bowl full.

As a pup she was totally unmanageable. If you put a collar and lead on her, she sat down and preferred strangulation to moving an inch against her will. She would not sit, stay or come if she did not want to. Our neighbor told us that if we beat her into submission (which entered my mind every waking minute of every single day that I was in contact with her) we would no longer have a "malamute" we would simply have "a dog", which sounded perfectly okay in my book.

She was about five months old when she experienced her first snowfall. We had been visiting Paul's parents in Fonthill, Ontario and since it was over a hundred miles each way, were staying the night. The late evening walk had been bone-chilling cold and by morning there was a foot of snow on the ground. Paul opened the front door and stepped out onto the balcony. Skeena took a couple of steps forward, dropped her head and stopped dead in her tracks. A front paw dangled in mid-air as she stared. The paw gingerly touched the snow and was pulled back instantly. She tried again. Suddenly the eyes widened, the ears pricked up and I swear I saw a light bulb go on over her head. She put her muzzle into the freshly fallen snow, spooning a little pyramid onto her snout and erupted.

She flew off the balcony all four legs splayed. She hit the pavement running from one side of the lawn to the other and back again. She raced down the sidewalk, across the road and

Free Spirit

back, jumping from snow pile to snow pile with Paul and me in hot pursuit.

We never came close to catching her. When we could no longer catch our breath we went back to the balcony and discussed trading her in on a Chihuahua. We now wished for some little creature that would quiver in these frigid climes and cross her paws, preferring to wait until the snow melted, before going outside.

We waited while Skeena ran the streets. We prayed that she would not meet a car or worse, a snow blower, now out in full force, head on. It took about forty-five minutes. She came tearing back, bounding up the stairs and throwing herself at Paul. She lay in his arms like a professional boxer that had just hit the mat, too tired to do anything but gasp. He carried the quaking mass into the kitchen where she bolted and hit the floor with a thud. She drank a huge bowl of water allowing the excess to dribble onto the floor, wolfed down her food and plopped herself on a throw rug in the corner. She was asleep before her head hit the linoleum. She lay there for hours reliving the joy of the great outdoors, moaning and twitching.

Since many of our friends and family lived hours away from our country home, we took Skeena along with us to most places, including a visit to Paul's Aunt Isabel living in Hamilton, Ontario. Aunt Isabel, in her mid-eighties, had been a concert pianist in her youth and since polio had confined her to a wheelchair, a couple of days each week was spent teaching teens the joys of the piano, in her home.

When we arrived we knocked, opened the door and our nine-month old, gigantic pup charged into the house. She ran from room to room until she found Aunt Isabel sitting on her bed. Skeena jumped up on the bed and instantly started pulling all the bobby pins out of her hair. Aunt Isabel let out one scream and Skeena was relegated to the back yard for the rest of the day, which was where she wanted to go in the first place.

For the years that she shared our lives we trained her as best we could and just enjoyed her antics. There was an endless supply of stories to tell. She had a wicked sense of humor and she knew it. The time she scared the hiker stands out vividly in my mind.

She needed no coaxing to get into the car. The minute the hatchback on the Honda Civic was lifted, she hopped in and settled down immediately in the small space between the back seat and the back door. We took her with us when we went walking on the Bruce Trail in Southern Ontario to see the changing of the leaves and to enjoy a taste of the brisk fall weather. Since there were only a few cars in the parking lot we assumed there would be few people on the trail. We let her off the lead. Although she was a fully-grown beast, she was gentle with people and only groundhogs took the full brunt of her wrath. Skeena led the way up the trail and stopped at berry patches to pluck the ripe fruit off with her lips as she waited for us to catch up. Close to the top she vanished.

We had no idea where she was until we saw some wild-eyed young man backing away from the bushes, shaking violently and mumbling "holy shit, holy shit." As he continued backing up, getting closer and closer to a deep crevasse, Skeena poked her head through the bushes, obviously for the second or third time. She knew she was scaring the hell out of the guy and loved her little prank. While he teetered on the edge, my husband spoke quietly so he wouldn't panic and jump.

"She's a dog," said Paul. "Look at her collar. Look at her collar. She's a dog," he repeated those words a few more times a little louder and a little more emphatic each time.

Free Spirit

Hearing a human voice, the guy calmed down slowly but Skeena's poor unsuspecting victim never took his eyes off her. She lowered her head and appeared to be laughing at him.

We couldn't help but chuckle to ourselves all the way down the hill.

Paws For The Comedienne

Part 2

One day, for no other reason than our own amusement, we decided to test Skeena's loyalty. It was a Saturday morning and we had slept in, deciding that this would be our day to do as little as possible. We were still in our bedclothes when Skeena came into our bedroom.

Trying to sound angry, I had Paul pinned against the wall, his hands and arms above his head. I was yelling and slapping the wall with my hand. Skeena jumped on me and barked in an effort to protect him. We were pleased with the results. Since Paul and I both drove the sixty miles into Toronto to work and our days were long and full of minor and major events, we waited until the following weekend to try again. This time we reversed the order. I should have known better. Paul had me pinned to the wall with one hand and angrily pounded the wall with his fist. Skeena went between his legs pushing him back slightly and jumped on me, helping him. I'm sure if there had been a genuine intruder, instead of my husband, Skeena would have seen that incident as a golden opportunity to eliminate me from her life. A guard dog for me she wasn't.

We ruled out guard dog pretty quickly. We also promptly ruled out hunting dog when a rabbit ran right by her nose and she just raised an eyebrow at it. She probably could have been a good working dog but she felt working was beneath her. Actually the job best suited to her talents was that of a comedienne. She thought she was hilariously funny.

We were out on the lawn when she discovered her first toad. She touched it with her paw and it jumped. This was great fun, she thought. She touched it again and again it

Free Spirit

jumped. She sniffed it and it sat there like a bump on a log. She nudged it with her nose and it jumped. The toad was a big, fat, juicy one and it revolted me. I tried to get Skeena away from it. She tried to pick it up in her mouth but I guess the taste was not what she anticipated. She dropped it and started to gag and spit.

"Let go of that dirty thing," I shrieked at Skeena.

Well she knew she had me. She picked up the toad by one or two toes and had the entire bloated body hanging out of her mouth. She would put it down momentarily to foam at the mouth, but the minute I approached she picked it up and ran. As soon as I ignored her she dropped it, gagged a few times and went back to her house to get some water. Needless to say, when I lost interest so did she.

During our short nights of television Skeena would sit by Paul's chair. Occasionally, when the spirit moved her, she would poke her cold, wet nose under his resting hand. Paul would reach down and pet the top of her head. A few minutes later she would poke him again and again he would reach down and pet her. She waited and would poke him again. She did this until Paul became aggravated with her and would try to slough her off by looking at her and saying "WHAT?" She would back off and wait. Then she would poke him again. Paul would put his face closer and closer with each poke finally saying "WHAT.....DO.....YOU.....WANT?" When Paul became most annoyed and he would be nose to nose with the dog, she would burp in his face. She would erupt into fits of laughter, bobbing around, jumping on and off furniture before finally chasing her tail in absolute ecstasy.

Although she was not your typical sporting dog she did love the water. On one winter outing near a lake she broke through the ice and was swimming around in a rather large hole close to shore. Paul managed to find some planking, laid it beside the hole and pulled her out by the scruff of her neck. She ran around madly shaking all the water off until she was dry and we were soaked and then jumped in again to finish the game she had started.

Winter or summer, the water was a real treat to her, however, drizzle a bit of shampoo onto her back and she howled like a banshee. So realistic was her performance that people around were sure she was suffering the tortures of the damned at the hands of the Marquis de Sade. In silence I endured the dirty looks I got.

Another treat for her was roaming our property and a jaunt in the woods for a few hours. She was allowed to do this only after our neighbors had penned their animals and fowl for the night. When we were ready for her to come home we would call. Most of the time she came back promptly. Occasionally we would have to resort to trickery. We turned on the popcorn machine and before the first kernel hit the top she was scratching at the door. Of course she insisted that we share and sat glued until we gave her a few. We presented her with them one at a time. If a particular large, white, fluffy popped corn missed the dabble of butter that she insisted be on every one, she spit it back at us.

If it got too late for popcorn we would yell for her to come back. The later the hour the harsher our voices became. When we were so angry she knew that if we caught her we would kill her, she would shoot past us, run into her kennel, close the door and hide in her house. All we could do was lock the door behind her.

Life with Skeena was never boring. She knew exactly what she wanted and accepted no less. She loved popcorn and ice cream and cold weather and swimming and playing catch with the plastic top of our garbage can and burying one of each of our boots and shoes in the snow. But mostly she loved Paul.

Free Spirit

They are together always.

Skeena
May, 1980 – September, 1989

Paul Gordon Hossack
February 27, 1940 –
June 26, 1992

1. A Candle to Light the Way
2. The Hands that Heal
3. The Date from Hell
4. Juno – A Love Story
5. Intimidation
6. The Race
7. Lonesome Traveler
8. Vive La Difference
9. Simple Act of Kindness
10. The Test of Time
11. Reflections
12. Some Day My Prince Will Come
13. I Was Not Supposed to be Here Alone

The Widowed Years

A Candle to Light the Way

"What are you doing back so soon?" Amy, my New Jersey friend, asked. "I thought you were going to be gone about four months."

"Did you get my letter from the American Embassy?" I asked, knowing full well that she couldn't have received it because of the question she asked.

"No," she answered. "What's happened?"

I took a deep breath, letting it out slowly knowing that I couldn't get through the next few sentences without breaking down into tears. "Paul had a heart attack in Germany and died without making it to the hospital. I'm having a memorial service in Toronto for him on July 14th and would like you and Norman to come."

I could hear her breathing. She said nothing. When she was finally able to talk, I could hear the sharp intake of air like she was fighting back tears, which immediately released a flood from me.

"We are in the middle of having lots of work done in the apartment. We have painters and workmen all over the place. Let me talk to Norman," she said. "One of us will come. Norman will call you back soon."

Paul and I had met Amy and Norman Prestup while camping in Rome. They had a sign in their window that said "English Books to Trade." We became friends almost immediately and traveled together through parts of Italy and Greece, celebrating Christmas and New Year together before separating on Crete when the Gulf War broke out. We stayed friends.

Free Spirit

Norman called within the hour. We talked for a long time before he said he would be coming to the service but added that he could only stay a short time. "I don't want to leave Amy alone with the workmen for too long."

"I have a better idea," I said. "I would really like to spend time with both of you and I know there won't be time before, during or after the service. Why don't you get the work done in your apartment and when you have time, pick me up in Toronto and take me camping with you? I know your heart will be with me at the service."

It was agreed.

The call came in mid-August. Amy said, "I don't care where we go, I just want to see a moose."

"Well, we'll have to head north then," I said. "It's been a while since I saw any wandering around in downtown Toronto."

Amy and Norman arrived a couple of days later after a two-day drive from Kearney, New Jersey. Since my brother, Harry, and his significant-other, Sandra, were in Montreal for a few days, I had their apartment to myself. Over dinner we studied the guidebooks and the camping books and decided on Miller Lake on the Bruce Peninsula. We called to make reservations and early the next morning, after coffee and toast, we were on our way.

I know we talked on the way up, but I really don't remember much of the conversation. With every lull in the conversation I would mist up with tears. As we got closer to our destination, Amy pointed to large cardboard billboard-like candles by the side of the road. I saw them and Amy told me later that I even commented on them, but nothing registered in my brain.

We found the campground and checked in. Since the Prestups don't like to be too close to civilization we found an out-of-the-way spot to set up housing for a few days. We made plans for dinner, which would be take-out pizza from the little souvenir/restaurant/mini-mart. We wandered around the shop to see if there was anything else we wanted or needed.

"You know," I said to Amy, "Paul and I came up here a few years ago. I think there's a candle shop within twenty-five or thirty miles from here. Let's plan on taking a trip out there. I became friends with the owner."

"Let's ask the lady where it is," Amy said.

"Excuse me," I said to the short, round woman behind the cash register. "Is there a candle factory up here some place?"

"Yes," she said and walked over to the window. "It's right over there," she said, pointing to a small house across the lawn, surrounded by a fence.

"No, no, no!" I said. "This is a big, candle factory I want to visit, not a little house," I said, showing my impatience.

"It's right over there," she repeated, pointing to the little house.

"No," I insisted. "They make candles right on the premises. I know the owner of the place and that's not it."

"Buddy?" she said.

"Buddy Albro," I repeated.

"It's right over there," she said again. "Buddy is the owner. I'll call him."

She called. The line was busy.

Amy came over to the window. "Why don't we walk?" she said. "It's right over there."

We took the path around the fencing and walked into the candle factory. Buddy had his back to me, but I still recognized his lanky body. "I didn't think you would still be here," I said.

Free Spirit

Buddy didn't even turn around when he said "Joei Carlton. We were just talking about you. How in the hell are you?"

We hugged before we said another word and I introduced him to Amy and Norman. I asked if he still spent his winters in California and he said, "No, we have a house on Siesta Key in Florida. Do you know where that is?" he asked.

"Well now, let me see," I said, "if I use my bicycle I can make it to Siesta Key in about fifteen minutes. I have a condo in Sarasota."

That night Buddy came to the Prestup motorhome to visit. To this day I don't remember laughing so hard over some of the things we had all been through. We renewed a five-year friendship from the time Paul and I first visited the candle shop. Amy and Norman absolutely fell in love with my charming and exceptionally witty friend. There were very few tears shed that night.

The next day Amy and I walked the entire campground. I was now more determined than ever that I wanted to get back into camping. "I have no idea what kind of vehicle I want," I said to Amy.

"Which one around here looks good?" Amy asked and I pointed to a motorhome that looked like a van similar to the one Paul and I had in Europe.

Before I realized what she was doing, she knocked on the door of the van. "My friend here is interested in purchasing one of these. Do you like it?" she asked.

They immediately introduced themselves and invited us into their camper. They pointed out all the cupboards and what they kept in each. Marge opened the door to the bathroom and showed how you could close off both sides for privacy. Jack told us about gas mileage and what great service he gets from the dealer, but he's had no problems with it at all. And they both loved it. We thanked them and left.

"Too small," I said before we reached the path.

"Okay, what else do you want to see," she asked.

By the time we got back to our spot, I had seen the insides of at least fifteen or sixteen motorhomes, vans and truck campers. "And no salesman will call," said Amy.

Over a barbecued dinner that night we discussed my future life. Whatever I wanted to do would have to wait until I was emotionally prepared to be on my own. The thought of going on without Paul was still very overwhelming so we talked about times past and the fun we had touring Europe.

We had five wonderful days of camping, sharing, laughing and crying and enjoying our friend Buddy. I knew then that I would get back into camping even if I had to do it myself.

On the drive back to Toronto we learned that Hurricane Hugo had come ashore and was devastating Homestead, Florida. The Prestups worried about their relatives living in the Miami area and I worried about my condo in Sarasota. After a few telephone calls from my brother's apartment we learned that all was safe.

I was back in Toronto about a week when I discovered a new brand of greeting cards called "From the Wilds of Canada." The front picture was that of an old woman holding onto a leash with a moose on the end of it sniffing a fire hydrant. That, I'm afraid, is the closest we came to a moose on this camping trip.

The Hands that Heal

To feel the warmth of someone's hands, a stranger's hands, yet gentle and familiar, with only a touch of longing as they caress and soothe and the last bit of tension evaporates.
"It's over," John whispered. "Relax."

* * * * *

"What a fabulous ploy," I thought as I knocked on the side door.

"Come on in," John shouted from the second story window. "I'll be down in a minute. Make yourself comfortable."

Finding a three-dimensional puzzle on the table in the waiting room my fingers fidgeted with the pieces until I found one that fit.

"Hi," said John. "Ready for your massage?"

"Yea, I think so," I replied as bravely as I could muster while my insides were turning to jelly.

"What the hell am I doing here?" the question kept rolling around in a mind that had ceased to function months ago. "I've never done this before. Why now?"

It had all started quite innocently the day before. I had seen John on several occasions in the office of the Marine Biology Lab where we both volunteered. He had always appeared shy, not talking much and until yesterday, had never spoken to me. When I did hear him speak, he spoke softly and always about projects going on at Mote Marine. I knew from the chitchat at the coffee breaks that he had lost his wife about the same time that I had been widowed. We shared a common sorrow, but while John was soft-spoken and gentlemanly I was loud and saucy. I talked about traveling. It was my current passion.

Joei Carlton Hossack

I took special notice of him the week before, when I sat behind him at the Monday morning briefing. The first time he had actually spoken to me was the day before.

YESTERDAY was the first time he spoke to me. He asked where my next trip would be. I told him I had promised my sister that I would stay in North America so we could visit for awhile. "I'll probably head for Alaska," I said, not really believing it. "I'd love to go someplace exotic like Viet Nam or Egypt." I told him about my new-found writing career and that I wanted something exciting and foreign to write about.

He told me about how he became a licensed massage therapist and "would you like a massage?" he asked as he handed me a business card. "Call me," he said.

"He's really cute," was all I could think about while we were up close and personal. I pointed and tapped my shoulders.

John started rubbing my shoulders gently but firmly. "I'll give you a week or two to stopped that," I quipped and didn't move for a moment in the hopes that he would continue.

"Thanks," I said far more nonchalantly than I felt. "That felt great," and left to start what would be long, busy day.

Sleep never did come easily but that night was one of the few good ones. I fell asleep feeling John's hands gliding smoothly over my neck and shoulders, fingers massaging sore muscles, slowing easing away the pain. I awoke the next morning feeling great and right after breakfast, I telephoned John before courage would fail me.

In three hours I would be lying naked on a massage table. With effort I pushed those thoughts to the back of my mind. I knew I wanted to enjoy life as I once had and to experience something new and different. I wanted to treat myself to all the fine things that this world had to offer before it was too late. I knew that it had been much too long since I experienced the healing powers of touch.

Free Spirit

The room was small, but warm and cozy. From the desk I picked up and examined a bottle of lotion while music played softly in the background.

"Take off whatever clothes you would feel comfortable taking off. Most people remove everything," John volunteered from the next room.

I wanted to cover up. I wanted to hide myself from the fifty-year-old body that belonged to me. But I didn't. "He is really cute," I thought for the hundredth time. "Do I really want him to see me this way?" It was just too late to back out. I stripped, putting my clothes neatly on the awaiting chair and crawled under the white sheet that was draped over the massage table.

A feeble "okay" and John came into the room.

Understanding my tension he was at my side issuing instructions until I said "ready" in a voice that was quietly hesitant. I closed my eyes.

Through nervousness I babbled on about the weather and travel and Mote Marine and anything else that popped into my mind but my first question was if he had just taken his hands out of the freezer? We laughed just enough to ease a little of the tension.

His hands were warm as he massaged my scalp, his thumbs pressing gently behind my ears and upper neck. I could feel his fingers sliding down the sides of my face. They soothed my forehead.

Before realizing what was happening and powerless to prevent it, tears filled my eyes and cascaded down the side of my face as John's hands continued to caress my temples, cheeks and finally my chin and neck.

"It's okay," he whispered softly. "It's just a release of tension. It's okay."

Joei Carlton Hossack

Every muscle was returning to life. His fingers gently massaged the back of my neck. He slid his hands under my shoulders and lifted my upper body ever so slightly.

"I'll do all the work," he said softly. "You don't have to move," and he slipped to my right side and uncovered an arm.

The lotion was warm and slippery and smelled of sea breezes. The entire length of my arm was stroked. The kneading started at the shoulder and slowly worked its way down to my hand, then each finger, and for a moment time stood still as I concentrated, never wanting it to end. He placed my arm back under the security of the cover and maneuvered effortlessly to the left side and started all over again from my shoulder.

Uncovering one leg at a time, the healing touch started at the top of my thigh, ending with my feet being rubbed and individual toes massaged until all the stress was gone. For brief moments the tension would ease, and each time it would bring uncontrollable tears. I had found a bit of heaven.

His hands were warm and moist with lotion and gliding over a body that for brief periods felt luxuriously mine. His fingers were kneading and manipulating, warming and caressing. Occasionally, for a brief moment I would stop talking long enough to feel the warmth and the sheer joy of being in a world of my own; however, as I would soon realize that I was naked, self-consciousness would return and I would be off babbling again. Gently but firmly, John rested his hands on my back, not moving. The massage was over. A glow descended over my body as I lay perfectly still, warmed by the experience of true pleasure.

"Why have I never done this before?" I wondered.

The Date from Hell

On a first date there is always a point, and it usually hits right at the beginning of the second mile, that you will NOT get out and walk home. We had just hit that spot when the topic of conversation which, for the previous minutes had included the weather, traffic problems and events of the day, changed abruptly.

"Everything you really need to know," he said without ceremony, "is in the Bible."

"Pardon me," I asked innocently, thinking I had heard incorrectly.

"Everything you really need to know," he repeated, "is in the Bible."

"What the hell are you talking about?" I asked, wrinkling up my nose and forehead so he would realize that I didn't appreciate where the conversation was headed. "How did we get from the news report of the archaeological digs in Egypt to the Bible?" I questioned, my voice taking on an unfamiliar and harsh tone. "Oh my God," I whispered through clenched teeth, "the date from hell."

* * * * *

I had met Carl several years before at the Community Park Association dance. He was an inch or so taller than I, mousy-brown unruly hair, with thick, tortoise-shell framed glasses and a pronounced limp. The only reason he had caught my eye was because he always seemed to be dancing and he definitely was amongst the younger men at the dance. We danced from time to time, nothing more.

On one particular Saturday evening we sat and talked. Traveling seemed to be the one thing we had in common so we

Joei Carlton Hossack

talked about places in the world we loved. I had spent my previous summer on three archaeological digs in England so we talked archaeology for awhile. He seemed so knowledgeable and for the first time in a long time I felt content to just sit at the table, munch some popcorn and pretzels, and talk. By the end of the evening we had talked the night away. I was not aware at that time that his knowledge came from books, magazines and the four newspapers that he read daily and not from actually getting on a plane and landing someplace exotic.

By the end of the evening I had confessed that I was a seasonal resident in Sarasota and would be leaving to go north by the end of the week. When he invited me to dinner, I accepted.

Carl called on Monday for dinner on Wednesday and I said yes. Although I wasn't ready for any involvement I felt the time was okay for a simple dinner. Besides, my refrigerator was practically empty and I had no intention of restocking. It seemed perfect.

He arrived on time, which was a good start. In my opinion he was overly dressed in a dark-gray suit and tie but it seemed appropriate for him. He held the car door open for me, which was another plus.

We headed out immediately. He talked about the weather at first and how he was delighted that it was warming up. He mentioned that he had a little trouble finding my place and would have been late except for the city map that he kept handy. Carl talked about the fact that he was an avid reader and that's when I discovered that he read four newspapers from cover to cover every morning and where he learned about the archaeological digs that were currently going on in Egypt. With each word, the car moved towards a local Thai restaurant, a favorite of mine.

Free Spirit

At this point in the very long-winded, one-sided conversation, we arrive at the point of no return, the two-mile marker, and conversation as I knew it, and had come to expect, ceased to exist.

"But," he said, "everything you really need to know is in the Bible."

"The Bible," I said my voice taking on the sound of a word totally foreign to me. "How the hell did we get from Egypt to the Bible?" I asked. It was definitely the wrong question to ask. When Carl started to explain, I politely changed the subject.

With every third sentence spoken, Carl mentioned the Bible. Changing the subject did not seem to help. Getting angry did not seem to help either. Nothing seemed to bother him. Nothing seemed to work. The man was wearing blinders and ear plugs.

The evening was a disaster. He talked and talked and talked, saying nothing that I wanted to hear. I said nothing. The evening ended right after dinner when I insisted on being taken home. I was relieved when he drove straight to my place. At the door I was rude, pure and simple. I thanked him for dinner and slammed the door of my condominium while he was still standing on the doorstep.

END OF STORY

Not on your life.

It was April fifteenth when I left Florida and headed north to Canada. I returned on November first and, as always, to a mountain of mail. During my six-and-a-half month absence, a package had arrived from Carl. I didn't have to open it to know what it contained but I opened it anyway. "All for me," I said sarcastically under my breath. "My very own Bible."

Since there was a return address on the small, brown envelope I sent him the following note: "When I return to Florida after six months of being away, I have enough junk mail to fill a large, black garbage bag. Your book is now part of that garbage bag."

I took the book and delivered it to the free, well-stocked library located in the clubhouse of the condominium. I knew that someone would cherish the book.

At the dance the following Saturday night I met up with Carl, who was most annoyed that I had destroyed the Bible. I never did confess. I loved the humor of it all. He'll have to spend the money to buy the book that this story is published in to find out what really happened.

Juno – A Love Story

She was such a tiny bit of a thing when she was stranded on July 17, 1994 on Juno Beach, Florida. Her mother watched from a distance as people gathered to help the little whale that was lying on its side on the sandy beach gasping for air. With the help of many people she was lifted, returned to the water and held at the surface while calls for help went out.

A local truck was dispatched immediately from the Fish and Game Authorities and Mote Marine Aquarium and Laboratory, on Florida's west coast, was notified to expect the infant and to prepare for her arrival.

While the baby whale lay motionless in the bed of the truck, with loving hands to sponge water over her body, the truck crossed central Florida. The entire trip took four hours and little Juno, as she was named because of the area of her stranding, arrived alive but gravely ill at the Marine Mammal Stranding Center, a part of Mote Marine, in Sarasota. Desperate calls for volunteers went out over the radio, television and newspapers. Thus begins the love story.

With the tank filled waist deep with water, Juno was surrounded by a rubber harness and gently lowered into the tank by a crane. Volunteers waited in the water to receive her. Loving arms held her at the surface while the top of her body was rubbed with zinc oxide to keep her skin from sunburning.

For twenty-four hours a day, in two-hour shifts, Juno was held at the surface so she would not drown. It was weeks before she was released to swim on her own for short periods of time to gain strength and even at those times, volunteers waited in the water. If she tired too quickly, she would sink to the bottom and not be able to come up for air.

Joei Carlton Hossack

    Initially, feeding her was another problem because she was the first live pygmy sperm whale stranding. Since Mote Marine was used to caring for dolphins, a baby dolphin formula was prepared. It did not take long for baby Juno to develop colic. Several different formulas produced the same results until the proper mixture was found.

    Marine mammals do not suckle. Juno was fed a ground fish mixture, combined with vitamins and antibiotics, through a tube which was put down her throat. Fortunately whales do not have a gag reflex.

    Each day that she lived she gained. She gained strength from the food. She gained health from the vitamins and antibiotics. She gained confidence by swimming. She gained and gave love to the hundreds of volunteers who helped and watched her daily. She gained much as the world watched and prayed for her.

    In the five months that she lived at Mote Marine she grew a foot in length and gained one hundred and fifty pounds in weight. Since she had lived in a hospital setting longer than she lived in the wild, preparations were underway for larger quarters. Juno would spend the rest of her life in captivity. Although she was a pygmy sperm whale, she would still grow to over a thousand pounds and would require much larger accommodations. As she grew bigger, stronger and more playful, so did the love for her grow and we all watched in fascination.

    At approximately five in the morning on January 11th, 1995 Juno started showing signs of major distress. Water was quickly lowered from her tank so the volunteers could go to her. The end was very sudden and very swift. She died in the arms of the only family she knew.

    I was one of the volunteers.

Intimidation

"What are you going to talk about?" asked the lady seated next to me. Although she was neatly dressed in a black silk pantsuit, her bandaged right leg was propped up on an ottoman and her cane rested on the floor beside her overstuffed chair, giving her a raggedy appearance.

"I spent three months traveling around Turkey in 1994, another month on a couple of Greek Islands and Cyprus, and I'm going to give a little presentation," I responded.

"Do you have slides?" she asked innocently.

"No," I explained, "this is just a lecture."

"Oh," she retorted, "three weeks ago we had a lady speak about her trip to Kenya. She had over two hundred slides to show us. There were slides of animals and plants and flowers and all kinds of different places she had photographed. Since you have no slides, do you have some pictures to show us?" she asked, her raised eyebrows creasing her forehead.

"No," I replied as confidently as I could while looking in every direction for any possible escape route. I was about to present my very first lecture and I suddenly had the feeling that I, rather than the audience, was standing there naked.

Six weeks earlier I had attended a singles' evening at the Jewish Community Center in Sarasota, Florida. The guests in the group were asked to introduce themselves and give a bit of personal history. This would not be a problem, I felt. I would give them my life in a nutshell.

When my turn came I stood and gave them my name. I told the group of about fifty or so people that I was a seasonal resident of Sarasota. I looked around the room as I advised them that I spend over six months each year traveling and that I am currently writing my first book, a collection of short stories. I smiled, nodded to a few individuals who were watching me intently, and sat down.

Before all the introductions were over the president of the singles' club approached me. "Would you like to give a lecture to our group?" he asked. "You can speak about any trip you want. Your choice."

The whole idea sounded intriguing. Since I had four months of Toastmasters (an international speaking organization) under my belt, it also sounded fairly simple. It would be marvelous practice, I thought. I accepted knowing that even though I had just returned from a driving/camping trip to Alaska, I would be speaking about one of my favorite parts of the world.....Turkey.

On the day of the lecture I did everything to shore up my confidence. I knew there would be questions and I hoped that by reading over my daily diary of the trip I would be able to answer them. I practiced my speech as best I could and tried to anticipate some of the questions.

For the occasion I dressed smartly and comfortably. I had prepared a few brief notes and had the start of my book on Turkey with me. I even had friends in the audience who had called to say they were going to be there just to lend support. I was fully prepared for everything.....everything, that is, except for this little lady seated on my right who had just told me that the last speaker had two hundred slides of Kenya. With her innocent smile, her creased forehead and mild-sounding words she had reduced my confidence level to that of the rank amateur that I was. I wanted to crawl under my chair.

The president called the meeting to order. I was introduced as the speaker for the evening. I thanked them for inviting me and immediately plowed ahead into my opening remarks.

Free Spirit

Since 1994 had actually been my third attempt at getting to Turkey, I read the start of my book that gave good background information. The neatly typed pages explained that in 1991 while on our way to Turkey, my husband Paul and I got "caught" on the Greek Island of Crete when the Gulf War erupted. The book touched briefly on the fact that in 1992, again on our way to Turkey, my husband had suffered a heart attack and died in a German campground. "To fulfill our dream I went to Turkey alone," I explained. I looked at the audience before going on.

"Although I was terrified," I continued, "I got off the plane at four-ten in the morning at the airport in Dalaman, Turkey and started an adventure that ended four months later. I loved the rugged countryside with its gorgeous beaches, the incredible tombs and fantastic archaeological sites, the deliciously spicy food and the kind, gracious people." Slides or no slides, I had them. They were listening.

The talk became a little less formal. Once I got into the swing of speaking in front of the group and knowing, by the look on their faces, that I had their full attention, it was thrilling. I relaxed enough to really enjoy the presentation. I even managed to stop and answer questions from time to time and had no problem getting back to the organized portion of the lecture that I had prepared.

A few members in the group of thirty knew that I had just returned from Alaska and while I talked about Ankara they wanted to talk about Anchorage. As gently as I could, and without the aid of a two-by-four I eased them back onto the subject. One hour and fifteen minutes later, after the odd yawn and the occasional extra-wide blink to keep their eyes open, I knew I was losing my audience. I ended quickly by saying "I would love to go back to Turkey some day. Does anyone want to go with me?"

Joei Carlton Hossack

The ensuing applause embarrassed me slightly. I nodded appreciatively. When it was all over I could feel the saliva returning to my mouth and quickly took a sip from the glass of water that had been placed on the table by my chair. My heart stopped thumping. We were all invited into the dining room where the table had been prepared with snacks and drinks.

After it was all over some friends approached. They complimented me on how confident I appeared and remarked on how much they enjoyed listening to my animated talk. It was only then that I confessed how intimidated I had been by the lady I heard about with the two hundred slides.

"Did you also hear that we asked her to stop showing the slides after the first hundred or so because it was so slow it was taking forever?" my friend Sunny Greenberg inquired.

"No," I replied.

"Did you also hear that when the lights were turned on after the slide presentation that most of the people in the audience were asleep?" she asked.

"No," I replied chuckling, "my little voice of doom didn't happen to mention that."

The Race

In view of the fact that I'm normally in great shape, I feel that it is my obligation to explain why I came in last.

It was a Friday night. A Singles' Valentines Day Party, organized by a local chapter of The American Cancer Society and for which I had paid roughly my monthly condo fee, was being held in one of the local posh hotels. From what I had heard, everybody who was anybody in Sarasota's elite crowd was going to be there. I was dressed to kill in a black, low-cut dress that showed all my curves and a fair bit of cleavage. I was on the dance floor for the first time that evening and just getting into the swing of it when the tuxedoed clod, dancing with a blond, giggling twinkie, twenty-five years his junior, crunched down on the side of my foot, midway across my arch. The entire dancing population heard my howl, as did the people sitting at the tables that ringed the floor. Fortunately the loud music kept my death scream from being heard at the police station fifteen blocks away. Mr. Clod uttered some inane apology. I muttered something back, I don't remember what.....and game over.

Saturday, not being able to get my shoe on, I sat at a small table loom and demonstrated my weaving skills at the Arts and Crafts Festival, held at the Sarasota Square Mall, along with several other members of the Weaver's Guild. Sunday was race day.

Over the years I had attended several 5k races. The money went to various charities like the Heart and Stroke Foundation, Cancer Research, AIDS Research and a few children's organizations. I loved the excitement and the camaraderie of it all and I always wore my free tee shirt

Joei Carlton Hossack

proudly. I usually attended the party afterwards, loading up on bagels and orange juice to replenish lost fluids. When a leg massage was offered I was one of the first in line. I enjoyed the whole ball of wax.

This was my first, and may I add only, 10k marathon. That was the day I learned that 10k was not double the distance of 5k. A walking distance of five kilometers is a pleasant stroll around a garden in a light refreshing mist while ten kilometers is walking on broken glass, barefooted through a steaming hot jungle and hopefully into the jaws of a waiting lion who will gladly put you out of your misery.

Despite my infirmity, I started strong. I walked with the others out onto the streets that circled the mall, each of us having been given a map of the high-class funeral procession. Police cars were lined up to protect the runners and walkers from the few cars that were out and about. One police car drove slowly behind the group to protect the last walker.

As the person behind passed me, my plight became apparent even it was only to me. Three miles into the marathon I had run, or should I confess, walked out of steam. The police car pulled closer.

"Hey Fuzz," I yelled, "either pick me up or run me down, please."

"You're looking great," was the response over the loud speaker. The officer behind the wheel sounded the bullhorn.

I continued walking. By mile four I was in agony.

"Hey Fuzz," I quipped, "am I starting to look slimmer?"

"Don't stand sideways," he said, again through the loud speaker. "You'll disappear. Looking great! Keep up the good work."

By mile five I begged them to shoot me. They answered with a couple of short blasts on the horn and a wave of the arm.

Free Spirit

I won't bore you with an inch-by-inch or even a mile-by-mile death march but when I staggered over the finish line, the police turned on the siren and had all their lights flashing. Everyone, the few people that were left anyway since the race had been long over, turned to look my way. Several cheered. A tiny second wind followed.

"I was in such trouble out there," I said. "Why didn't you pick me up when I begged you to?"

"Because as long as you were talking we knew you were okay. If you had stopped walking and waved we would have picked you up instantly."

Moral to the story: Learn when it is essential to keep your mouth shut.

Lonesome Traveler

My stomach was in a knot that squeezed tighter and tighter and my head pounded like someone was hitting it with a hammer. "Never drive when angry" kept coming to mind but what was I to do? I needed to remove myself from the situation as soon as possible or go completely berserk. I needed the comfort of my friends and family so I drove angry.

The person I had rented my condominium to had stopped payment on the last month's rent check. When I learned that my air-conditioner had died one muggy, Floridian day and could not be repaired, I drove back to my condo from New Mexico to check it out. Since I was told that the tenant had moved, I went into the condo as soon as I arrived. He had moved. His belongings had not.

My home was a mess. He had piled his furniture on top of mine and what couldn't be "piled on" was put out onto my un-air-conditioned lanai to grow mold. His cat, which he had forgotten to mention even after I told him 'no pets' had used one of my kitchen drawers as a cat bed or worse. When I called my tenant at work to tell him to get his things out of my home, he returned that evening, changed the lock, and refused to leave until the lease was up.

My neighbor, directly across from my condo, allowed me to stay in her guest room since I really had no place to stay without renting an apartment or a room someplace. I watched from the bedroom window as he taunted me with his comings and goings.

With just a few articles of clothing, my toiletries and my credit cards, I left my neighbor's home around noon and headed north. I drove to Valdosta, Georgia stopping only for gasoline. Driving usually relaxed me and this was no exception but I still

Free Spirit

felt far from my buoyant self. I felt displaced, despondent and homeless. I would have to fight to get my home back.

I cursed myself for having rented it to him in the first place. "Why had I done it?" I said to myself over and over, trying not to grind my teeth in the process. He was newly divorced, desperately in need of a reasonable place to stay, and I was leaving for the summer. These three elements, combined, would prove to be my downfall, I felt.

My choice for a motel room that night was a poor one. The room was spacious, clean and provided all the amenities but it was well back in the motel lot and there were not many people around. I was nervous and didn't really want to drive to go out to dinner but I had no choice. As much as I would have enjoyed a bit of exercise, a lengthy walk in the dark in an unfamiliar area did not appeal to me.

Dinner was tasteless even though I took special pains to order one of my favorite meals.....jumbo fried shrimp. It had been a long day of driving and now I was alone and agitated. I ate a few shrimp and my salad and took the rest back to the room in the hopes that I would nibble at the rest. I didn't. There was nothing that held my interest on television. I slept fitfully that night, but I slept.

The next day was another long drive-day. I stopped twenty miles south of Lexington, Kentucky and made a much better choice of hotel. I took an hour to close my eyes, letting the television set drone in the background. A long, slow, relaxing bath, allowing the hot water to drain every bit of stress from my body before dressing for dinner, did wonders as well.

The Cracker Barrel Restaurant was located right across the parking lot from the hotel and was crowded. Seeing all the people milling around took my mind off my problems for a while. I gave my name and the number in my party to the hostess. The name directly above mine was a single as well.

Joei Carlton Hossack

I shopped. I browsed. I handled each piece of merchandise as though I was fascinated by everything in the hopes of killing some time. I waited. The longer I waited the more agitated I became. I wanted to talk to someone…..anyone. I checked the list.

Perhaps the people whose names were on the list after my name said they wanted smoking but both the name ahead of mine and mine were skipped over. A man was approaching.

I screwed up my courage and before I lost my nerve I said quickly "we both seem to be dining alone in the non-smoking section. Would you care to share a table?"

The change on his face was immediate and dramatic. His eyes suddenly glowed. He gave me a big smile, showing lots of white, straight teeth. He was as thrilled with the prospect of a dinner companion as I was. We were chatting even before we arrived at our table, which they showed us to immediately.

"I'm heading south," he said. "I was visiting my daughter and grandchildren in Toledo for a few days. I miss them and it's so far from Atlanta. I see them only a couple times a year now."

"I spend my winters in Florida," I confided, "but my family live in Montreal and Toronto. I miss them also but I spend six months of the year traveling. I have a condo in Sarasota."

"We live in a seniors residence in Atlanta," he said.

"We?" I asked, "Your wife doesn't drive with you to see your children?"

"No," he replied, a touch of sadness in his voice. "She has Alzheimer's and doesn't recognize anyone anymore."

"I'm so sorry. It must be terribly difficult to deal with. How long have you been married?" I asked.

"Fifty-one years."

Free Spirit

"That's how old I am," I said. "Fifty-one years. A lot can happen in fifty-one years. I have been widowed for three of those years."

"I'm sorry," he said. "I know that I shouldn't be telling you this but I now have a lady friend. I cannot tell my daughter. She wouldn't understand."

"I know it's lonely," I said. "And you have to take the joy where you find it. I'll find it again some day I think."

"I know you will," he said. "You're a very pretty lady. Where did you travel to this year?" he asked, opening an entirely new theme to the conversation.

"I drove to Alaska," I said. "I cannot believe how much driving I will have done this summer by the time I get back to my home. If I get my home back," I said almost under my breath.

"What do you mean 'if you get your home back?'" he asked.

The conversation never stopped. The hour and a half of sharing had changed my mood, my outlook, my entire day, in fact and only at the end of the meal did we introduce ourselves. We thanked each other as we said our good-byes in the parking lot and shook hands. We wished each other a safe journey and parted.

Would it be so difficult, particularly in areas of high travel, to have one table with four, six or eight chairs set aside for people traveling alone and who would like to share conversation with other lonesome travelers?

Vive La Difference

Part 1

"You're going to have to leave your little girlfriend now and come inside," she said to her husband just loud enough for me, the campground, the bordering counties, the adjacent states and a foreign country or two, to overhear.

"Little girlfriend! Little girlfriend!" The words touched every raw nerve ending before echoing around in my brain until I wanted to scream. That "little girlfriend" the woman was talking about was me and I was certainly nobody's "little girlfriend."

This was my first night in a nearly empty campground, traveling by myself, on a journey that I knew would last about six months. "What an awful way to start," I thought. As the frustration and anger subsided I suddenly felt sick at heart.

I had left the home of my friend, Pat Thomas in Beeton, Ontario that morning. By late afternoon I had crossed the border at Sarnia into Port Huron, Michigan. The border guard, with all of his questions about why I was traveling alone, while staring steadily at me without a hint of friendliness, had already intimidated me. I wanted to stop early.

Why I was traveling alone had already brought tears to my eyes and a lower lip that had started quivering. I didn't need "Where are you going? What are you bringing into the country? How long will you be staying?" There was a whole rash of questions that had never been asked of me before and brought me to near panic. The more visibly upset I became, the more questions he asked before finally peering through my window into the van and waving me on.

Free Spirit

I pulled into the parking lot of a small grocery store. I had a good cry, dried my eyes and washed my face before heading inside to pick up a few essentials. I drove on and started looking for an open campground. I needed to get organized early. I hadn't figured out yet how everything worked in the motorhome. The van was relatively new and a bit complicated to me. I not only had to prepare dinner on a tiny two-burner stove but I had to figure out how the table was set up and try to remember where I had hidden all the kitchen paraphernalia. When all that was done, I had to pop the top on my Volkswagen Westphalia, something I had done only one or two times before. It took a little practice because the wraparound canvas was the only thing protecting me from the elements and I didn't want them snagged. I also had to unpack the groceries that I had purchased and to figure out where everything could be stored with so little storage space.

"Besides" I mumbled into thin air, "where the hell am I going in such a hurry?"

It was just the middle of May and only a few campgrounds were open for business. The first open park I came to, after crossing the border into the United States, was Lakeport State Park.

After paying the entrance fees into the park and an additional eight dollars in camping fees at the main gate, I drove around the park. With so few people it looked bleak and empty. I pulled into one of the numerous vacant spots. Since my campervan had only basic facilities, I chose a spot close to the rest rooms and showers. I turned off the faceless voice droning out of the radio that had been my company for the day.

I leveled the van as best I could, turned the motor off and breathed a huge sigh of relief. Like it or not I was home for the night. I sat immobilized for a few moments never letting go of the steering wheel. My unseeing eyes stared straight ahead.

Joei Carlton Hossack

It didn't take long before I could feel the first uncomfortable stirrings of depression. I had to move before the blackness took hold or got worse.

I got out of the van, locking the doors and checking to make sure that the hatchback was secure as well. Within minutes I had made a visual summary. The place was clean and tidy and disappointingly devoid of people. There was, however, a large group of people in the camping site opposite me. To accommodate their entire clan they had taken my picnic table. A few waved to greet me. When one of the young, sturdy members of the group offered to return the picnic table immediately I said, "I won't be using it so there's no rush."

After plugging in my electricity and popping the top, which was certainly easier than I had remembered, I went for a walk. I ambled along the paved path in the campground and hiked the fringe of the wooded area that ran around the back where the tenters would be parked, if there were any, until I felt relatively peaceful. Thankfully I also felt the beginnings of a hunger pang.

I had made it through my first day of driving with just a few tears. Alaska, my ultimate destination, was a trip that my husband Paul and I had planned on taking together. He had been an avid fisherman. He had loved the outdoors. He used to dream of pulling giant salmon out of Arctic waters, even larger than the thirty-five pounder he had pulled out of Lake Ontario and had hung so proudly on the wall of our den. Paul was gone now. This was just one of the trips that I felt I had to take alone. Mistakenly I felt that accomplishing some of our goals would ease some of the pain.

The walk had cleared my mind slightly. I sauntered back to my spot to busy myself preparing dinner. With the help of a brand new pressure cooker, the chicken in broth over rice with a variety of sliced and diced vegetables did not take long to

Free Spirit

prepare. Eating alone, however, was entirely another matter. If I was going to enjoy the next few months, I thought, I had better get used to doing many things alone.

I ate in silence with a book propped open on my lap. I sat slumped in my deck chair just outside my sliding side door resting my outstretched legs on the step of the van. I tried to concentrate on the novel, making a special effort not to dribble my food down the front of my shirt. I was glad when dinner was over and I didn't have to sit there pretending I was enjoying everything anymore.

As I was putting the last of the dinner dishes away, the elder in the group camping across from me called and motioned for me to come over.

"Are you alone?" he asked, sure that I was. "Bring your chair over to the fire and sit with us a bit."

I did not need much in the way of encouragement. I thanked him, returned to my outdoor spot, folded up my chair and carried it over to the fire. I smiled at each one in the group, nodded a greeting and introduced myself. A few looked my way and smiled as I unfolded my chair in a spot as close to the bonfire as I dared. With outstretched hands and fingers I luxuriated in the warmth of the crackling fire. It felt wonderful since the early evening dampness had crept into the air.

The older members of the group, I learned, were the only paid occupants at the campsite. All others were visitors: three daughters, two husbands, children and a few friends from a neighboring town. The conversation was relatively subdued but all seemed to get along well and none seemed terribly concerned that I had joined them. They did not say much to me. I just listened.

As night descended it got colder. Most of the guests said goodbye and left, taking with them picnic items, deck chairs, clothes, toys and scattered bits and pieces. The wife of the old man left without saying a word and joined another family of campers at their campsite. I sat listening to the old man and his crony. The conversation went in one ear and out the other without stopping, detouring or peaking my interest. Since I was being ignored anyway, I sat lost in my own thoughts, roasting the front of my body.

"Besides," I sighed, keeping my thoughts to myself "if I left now I would be sitting alone in my van." I was not quite prepared for that. Although it was quite dark, the evening was still early and the fire was warm. I stayed saying nothing.

When his friend left, Jim, as he now introduced himself, turned his attention to me. The reason for the family gathering, he explained, was due to his illness. His body was swollen with cancer and from the chemotherapy, he said. He anguished over the swelling in his legs, focusing on the fact that he could hardly walk. He was depressed over the loss of the few strands of hair that he had left before the chemo. He talked quietly while I listened.

When he asked why I was traveling alone I told him about the death of my husband.

It was at that time that his wife returned and remarked "you're going to have to leave your little girlfriend now and come inside."

"I'll be in shortly," he said.

She repeated herself giving me a cold, hard stare. My heart shriveled.

"I'll be there soon," he said sounding angry, "I want to keep talking to my friend."

I suddenly wanted to run back to my camper or better yet have the ground open up under my chair and swallow me whole. We never did get back to our conversation and I was glad because I was so close to tears. Except for the border guard, these were the only people I had spoken to all day. I said

Free Spirit

good night softly and walked away quickly. My eyes filled with tears before I could unlock the side door and climb inside.

I took down the sheets and blankets that had been stored on the upper bed and arranged the pillows already on the bench seat that converted to my bed. I turned on my black-and-white television set and allowed it to drone in the background not knowing or caring what was playing. I crawled into bed and allowed the tears to come, hoping for exhaustion and blessed sleep.

My mind worked overtime. I had lost a beautiful, fifty-two-year-old husband to a heart attack, so naturally I wanted to run off with a seventy-year-old, three-hundred-pound man suffering from cancer. "How could I resist?" I spat the words out sarcastically under my breath. "Little girlfriend indeed" suddenly feeling angry before the next crying jag hit.

The next morning everyone milled around at the camping spot across from me. While they busied themselves with breakfast, I cleaned up, packed up and left without saying a word to anyone. No one made an attempt to say goodbye or even wave to me as I pulled out.

I spent much of the day contemplating the events of the previous evening. I cried a bit because I was sure that this sort of pettiness and my own unhappiness would plague me, to various degrees, all the way to Alaska and back. When I wasn't feeling sorry for myself I was laughing at the fact that as a fifty-year-old, gray-haired, thirty-pound overweight woman, the old hag considered me a vamp who would run off with her man.

Vive La Différence

Part 2

The more I thought about the unpleasant incident, the more I was reminded of the trip that I had taken the previous year. I had spent four months traveling solo through Turkey, the Greek Islands and Cyprus. One particular incident produced a smile and calmed my jangled nerves almost immediately.

I had discovered the most charming and colorful little resort town of Kaş on the coast about half way between Istanbul to the north and Syria to the south. The area was called the Turquoise Coast because of the sparkling, azure color of the water. The scenery was breathtaking with Turkish and Greek Islands dotting the water so close that you felt like that you could swim out and touch them. The food was richly spiced and as tasty as I had ever experienced. It was served mostly in mini-bites or plastered onto freshly baked bread, which I loved. The locals were friendly and easily approachable. The town was filled with tourists, but everyone, local and tourist alike spoke some degree of English. I felt at home and used Kaş as my base. Since everyone had their own story to tell, I had no problem meeting people and making friends and exchanging histories.

On most days, I had my breakfast at a small outdoor restaurant called Café Corner. Abdullah or Apo as the people who knew and loved him called him, was a tall, dark, handsome and charming twenty-year-old. He was my waiter. He took all orders with a certain flourish that guaranteed him a good tip, but the younger and prettier you were, the more attention he

Free Spirit

lavished on you. When the young and pretty weren't around he flirted shamelessly with whoever was there.

I gave Apo the order for my yogurt breakfast, a real treat. It consisted of a layer of fresh fruit, a layer of yogurt and topped with honey and chopped nuts. A large cup of appletea accompanied the order. When my breakfast was served, a couple seated at the next table eyed it admiringly and the conversation started almost immediately.

"Yes, it's wonderful," I said. "I have it almost every morning. You never know what kind of fruit is on the bottom. I guess they pick up what is cheapest for the day and slice it up. I love it."

They both ordered the same.

From their accent I know they were from England and they introduced themselves as Margaret and Lyle. They could not decipher my accent and after telling them my name, I explained that I live part of the year in the United States, part of the year in Canada and somewhere in between I travel the world for six months at a time.

By the time we had discussed where we were from, what we had seen in Turkey, how long we had been visiting, where we were staying, with jokes added to an already spiced conversation, many hours had passed. Perhaps it was the hectic afternoon, breakfast and morning long since gone, of drinking tea, talking and laughing or the fact that the temperature was one hundred and twenty degrees plus, that made us feel we deserved a rest. Before heading back to our respective rooms for a mid-afternoon nap, they suggested that we meet later that day for dinner. I accepted.

Since the rooms were just as hot as the outdoors, we were all regrouped at Café Corner by early evening. I introduced my friends to another refreshing treat, a drink of sour cherry juice (vişne) and soda over ice. We relaxed over a couple of them before going to dinner at their favorite restaurant on the main street of the town. The dinner, consisting of side dish plates of grilled eggplant, green beans with almonds, humus and black olives, was served before the lamb shish kabob and was mouth-watering delicious. We spent hours talking and telling jokes, the naughtier the better. Once I got started, and had an audience who enjoyed my humor, I dredged up the jokes and stories going back to my (and everyone else's) childhood. It got funnier when we all knew the jokes and laughed before the punch lines.

During dinner Margaret mentioned that some close friends would be arriving the next day from England. "We want you to meet them. They are dear friends and I know you'll love them," she went on. "Let's meet at Café Corner in the afternoon and then we'll decide where we'll go for dinner."

I was surprised and delighted with the invitation and was not shy in mentioning it. "This would rarely happen in America," I said. "Single woman are usually shunned by couples," I told them.

"Listen," said Margaret. "I've been married to this old fart for thirty-five years. "I know everything that is going to come out of his mouth long before he says it. You, My Dear, on the other hand are refreshing and funny and cheery and I know our friends would love to meet you."

"Thank you, yes" I replied, "I would love to meet your friends and join you for dinner." The evening ended late. After dinner at the restaurant, we went back to Café Corner for a few more drinks and then on to another restaurant for coffee. I'm not sure who found the last restaurant but we were at the back of the restaurant on a dark side street with only locals around.

That evening and the next were some of the many highlights of my trip to Turkey. There were five of us for dinner that next night and the new arrivals, Richard and Cleo,

Free Spirit

matched my jokes with some I had never heard before. I could not remember when I had laughed so hard or for so long.

What a change, I thought, from my night in the State Park. I had always assumed that campers were a friendly lot. It hurt to be wrong.

I pointed my van and headed westward. The miracle of Christmas is an every day event in the German town of Frankenmuth, Michigan. That's where I would stop next.

Simple Act of Kindness

I was just beginning to get used to traveling alone but it still got lonely at times and it was not always easy keeping myself buoyed up and in the right frame of mind to meet people. The time of year was a difficult one as well. The previous day had been the third anniversary of my husband's death. I was now wandering through Yellowstone National Park before returning to my camping spot in Colter Bay, Grand Teton National Park.

I still had about twenty-five miles to drive when the rain started, slowly at first. It was just spitting in fact. The intermittent windshield wipers took care of the problem but only momentarily. Within seconds I found myself driving under a horrendous black cloud that had ripped open and no matter how fast my windshield wipers worked, they could not keep up with the deluge. The change was startlingly sudden.

I could hardly see where I was going and, with no warning, my right wiper started causing problems. The passenger-side wiper still worked, but not in sync with the other one. One touch from the out-of-kilter wiper and the driver-side started going haywire. "My God what's happening!" I screamed as if there was someone there to hear me.

The rain increased, as if that were possible, and the roads became treacherous with murky water and sludge forming pools in the center of the road. With my heart pounding so hard my ears hurt, I pulled off the road onto a small muddy rest area. There was no one else on the road.

I started to panic. I could feel the tears welling up in my eyes. It wasn't even night yet and it was so dark I needed my headlights just to see the road ahead. I forced myself back on

Free Spirit

the road. I shifted into second gear and inched my way, getting up to about twenty miles an hour. I turned my wipers on only when I really couldn't see and, even then, letting them swipe at the window only once. The passenger-side wiper finally flopped over one last time and died.

Each time I turned the wipers on I whispered a prayer, "please let me get through this nightmare."

As if by magic, the minute I left Yellowstone National Park and entered the Grand Teton, the sun came out. Glorious, bright, warm sunshine. I felt safe. Still shaken by the fierceness and velocity of the storm, I kept moving, picking up a little speed and hoping it wouldn't catch up to me again. I found the campground and my site. As soon as I turned off the motor and took a couple of deep, cleansing breaths, my heart stopped pounding.

I relaxed with a cup of herbal tea and started preparing dinner. My stomach was still a bit queasy but once relaxed, I knew I would need something light and soothing for dinner. While my homemade bean and vegetable soup simmered in my pressure cooker on the stove, I checked my manual. There was a Volkswagen dealership in Jackson, Wyoming, forty miles south of Grand Teton National Park. I breathed a sigh of relief. Not only would I get my windshield wiper repaired, but Jackson and Jackson Hole were on my list of must-see places.

After an early breakfast, I headed directly for the dealership in Jackson. The VW dealer had become a GEO dealer. I asked if the VW dealer had moved to another part of town.

"No," said the young executive sitting at a desk behind the glass window. "What's the problem?" he asked seeing the distress in my eyes.

I explained my floppy wiper problem as best I could.

"I had a VW once," he said. "Let me check it."

Joei Carlton Hossack

With a small wrench he tightened the bolt at the base of the wiper. He guaranteed that it would solve the problem. "The wipers on the VW are designed to loosen before they damage the motor," he explained

I turned them on. The passenger side did indeed work. When I offered to pay, he held up his hand. "No problem," he said.

In my moment of quiet relief, I forgot to mention that the bolt on driver's side wiper could use a little twist as well. Shortly after leaving the GEO dealer I tested them. My wiper was a little slow and floppy but it still worked.

"Never mind," I said out loud, grateful to be aware of how easy it was to correct. "I'll have it fixed at my next gas fill up."

I took the long, scenic route back to Colter Bay after stopping in Jackson for a couple of hours to wander the main streets, check out the designer shops and the city park before picking up an ice cream cone and getting on the road. I stopped en route to enjoy the spectacular scenery and a bit of lunch.

Eons of glaciers and earthquakes, according to my guidebook, had produced the Teton Range and while I watched the landscape, black clouds started to engulf the mountains. While I stood in cool sunshine, I observed through binoculars, a raging blizzard cover the highest peaks on the mountain. When the first droplets pelted my face, I returned to the van and drove on.

I stopped one last time because a large crowd had gathered by a stream. I took out my binoculars and observed a mother and baby moose walking knee-deep, drinking and munching as they slowly headed towards us.

Safely back at the campground, I watched as a mother, father and three boys moved into the site behind mine. They unloaded a motorbike and within minutes mother and youngest

Free Spirit

son belched away leaving a stream of black smoke and the rest of the crew to start setting up camp.

When mother and son returned, the two older boys took a spin on the bike. When they returned, father and one son whizzed by and disappeared around the corner. The motorbike mambo went on for over an hour and when I saw an opportunity, I approached the father.

"You know," I said after pointing to my camping site and introducing myself, "I have never known anyone who owned a motorbike that did not have a complete set of ratchet tools."

"Dan Strevey," he said breaking into a warm smile, "what do you need?"

While he tightened my windshield wiper we talked about the park and the camping spots and the weather and without a hint of warning, he asked a direct question. "Are you in there alone?"

Although I did not want my solo travels to be common knowledge, I nonetheless said "yes."

"Join us for dinner," he said.

I thanked him for fixing my wiper and for the dinner invitation. At six o'clock, when I saw his wife outside preparing their evening meal, I approached. "Are you aware that your husband is inviting strange women for dinner?" I asked.

"Yes," she answered, introducing herself as Jacque, "and we are expecting you." Before resuming KP duties she introduced me to sons, Scott, Jack and Daniel.

I joined them at their picnic table, bringing along a huge pot of piping hot, homemade soup and the remains of a bottle of wine. We gathered around the table and started dinner with my soup offering and fresh bread that I had picked up at the supermarket in Jackson. We had spaghetti, salad and dessert.

Joei Carlton Hossack

When my wine bottle lay like a dead soldier, Dan opened one of theirs.

We told travel stories and shared our experiences in the wild. Just before dark the ghost stories started. As night fell we moved closer and huddled around the crackling bonfire. When we had consumed more food and drink than was reasonable or necessary at any one meal, I was introduced to s'mores…..a toasted marshmallow flanked by pieces of minted chocolate and sandwiched between two graham crackers. It was sweet enough to keep any dentist in business the entire length of his career but absolutely delicious.

This simple evening with a wonderful family is one of my treasured memories on a trip that started with a frightened, but determined gray-haired woman from Sarasota, Florida and ended almost twenty-five thousand miles and six-and-a-half months later with the world by the tail…..and a tale to tell the world.

The Test of Time

The face was exactly as I had remembered, a little older perhaps, but the same face. She was still slim. Her dark hair was neatly coifed and she was stylishly dressed in a dark gray pantsuit. She stood at the deli counter waiting to place her order while talking to a friend.

"It cannot be her," my mind said but I stood there fascinated. "It's been over forty years. Surely she would have changed to the point where I wouldn't recognize her. Over forty years!"

Waiting at the same counter, I watched, taking it all in and having my mind go back to grade five, watching my favorite teacher standing at the head of the class and patiently instructing in English or reading or arithmetic or health. Was she beautiful? Of course, she was beautiful.

Before graduating into the next class, which for me meant a new school, she wrote in my diary: "May you always be as helpful to the next person as you are to me. June, 1954, Anne Harrison." I was ten years old at the time. I was not a pretty child. I was not a bright child. The words in my diary meant the world to me.

The years passed. I grew tall and lean and, yes, pretty. I also discovered somewhere along the way that I was bright. In the years that followed, the only news I heard of my fifth grade teacher was in my late teens when I was living away from home for the first time. My mother informed me, over the phone, that Miss Harrison had gotten married. Although my mind remembered that lovely woman and the words in my diary, my mouth said, "that old lady got married." Several weeks later the newspaper clipping announcing the nuptials arrived in the mail from my mother and I had a good hearty laugh. "That old lady" was perhaps around thirty years old.

Suddenly she and her friend were walking out the front door of the deli-restaurant. In a flash I returned to the present. I paid for my purchase and ran out the door. I stopped her friend and asked if the woman she had been talking to was Anne Harrison Lerner. She said "yes." I thanked her and ran off to catch up to my beloved teacher. In that same instant she disappeared. I looked into each store before I spotted her at the counter of the shoe repair. I waited a good distance from the door so I wouldn't frighten her when I approached.

"Mrs. Lerner," I said walking towards her.

"Yes," she replied raising her brows to show sparkling dark eyes.

For a moment I felt like that awkward ten-year-old when I told her that she had been my fifth grade teacher. "Joei Carlton" I said before she could ask and within a split second I confessed that in all my years of going to school she had been my favorite teacher. Without stopping for a breath, afraid that I would become self-conscious, I told her of the message she had written in my diary and that in low moments had given me strength. The awkwardness passed and she asked what my life was like now.

"I am a wanderer," I said. "I travel. I tell stories and I write."

"My daughter is a writer," she said "and she loves it."

"Yes, I must confess, I love it also. Do you still teach?" I asked.

"No, my husband likes me at home so I took early retirement," she said. "You were in the first class I ever taught. I was seventeen years old and had a one-year teaching degree. I taught for thirty-five years and loved every minute of it. I like being at home now," she confided. "We are close to our

Free Spirit

daughter and our granddaughter and being home gives us a chance to see them often."

The years slipped by as we talked, going from student and teacher to woman and woman. We said our good-byes and I promised I would call on my next trip to Montreal. I watched as she walked towards her car and waved one last time.

I turned and went back into the shopping center where I was meeting my brothers for dinner. As I walked towards our meeting spot I passed a mirror. "Cripes," I thought, running my fingers through my hair as I looked at myself in the mirror. Would I want some gray-haired lady walking up to me saying, "you were MY teacher about a million years ago."

Was she beautiful? Of course, she was beautiful. The years never touch the insides.

Reflections

I'm not sure if it happens to me at this time every year or if it just fell on me like a ton of bricks this year. There doesn't seem to be any apparent reason for it. This is no more of a milestone on this calendar year than any other year. There is no monumental birthday coming up, since I feel that the best ten years of a woman's life are between the ages of fifty and fifty-one. There is no special anniversary around the bend that should produce any more stress this year than last. Something just doesn't feel right and I can't put my finger on it. And to make matters worse, it just hit me out of nowhere.

The date was January 2nd, the year unimportant, and I was strolling around the Escapee campground in Livingston, Texas hoping for a little exercise. I was saying "hello" or nodding and waving to people as they passed and realizing that I just didn't want to be here. Unfortunately, I didn't have a clue as to where I would prefer to be.

My mind just traveled back to the beginning. Since leaving the comfort of my home and job and country in 1989, I have seen and experienced much. I have traveled more of the world than I ever imagined. I have walked in places that Jesus and Paul and their followers walked. I have dug up ancient and long-dead cities. I have touched the stars in the heavens on the other side of this planet. I have driven on the top of the world.

I have eaten meals with people who did not speak my language and yet we understood each other. I have cooked in kitchens so small that I didn't have to move my feet to get whatever I needed. I have laughed at some of the silliest predicaments I found myself in. I have cried almost every day over some of the losses in my life. I have prayed for peace for

Free Spirit

myself, my family, my friends and for anyone needing help. My heart has been overjoyed at some of the wonders I have seen, and when I run into a familiar face anywhere in my travels, I just want to hug them. I have been alone in strange countries and have stood in awe. I have been alone in strange countries and have been terrified.

In the past five years my life has changed to something I don't recognize anymore. I travel. I write. I lecture. I let my audiences know how fabulous it is to be living on the road without a home to go to. I joke about the challenges. I kid about the frustrations. I talk about the camaraderie and friendships and the magnificent sights in little hideaway places. I'm just not sure I believe it anymore.....or maybe I just needed to spout off. Thanks for listening.

I still haven't found a life that I like better than the one I'm living one day at a time.

Happy and prosperous New Year to you'all.

Some Day My Prince Will Come

I had had an amazing night's sleep and for the first time in seven months that great night's sleep was in my own bed, in my own house, in Sarasota, Florida.

After fidgeting, fussing and fuming for forty-one hours on a bus from Toronto, Canada to Sarasota, I had actually slept in and crawled out of my bed at eight o'clock in the morning. Never had I slept so peacefully or so long.

Groggy and still in a bit of a daze I shuffled my way into the kitchen. I found my coffee maker sitting at the back of one of my kitchen cupboards and gently lifted it out. I allowed the water to run for a bit and watched as it went from a rusty-red to only slightly murky, the typical color of Sarasota water. I washed and rinsed out the pot. I put it back in the usual place on the counter. I took the coffee out of the refrigerator, opened the new canister of Don Francisco's Vanilla Nut, my favorite, and measured out a couple of heaping tablespoons, dumping them into a new filter. I filled the trough with water and just as I was about to switch it on I heard a soft thud.

"What the hell was that?" I mumbled as I turned and looked at the floor, hoping I hadn't dropped anything breakable.

I stared in disbelief and disgust. "How the hell did a frog, the size of my hand, get into my kitchen?" I wondered. "Who cares how he got in," I mumbled. "What am I going to do about him."

A variety of distasteful choices popped into my mind. The first of which was to pick up the little guy, give him a great big kiss and see if he turns into the Prince of Sarasota. With my luck he would turn into the typical, Floridian playboy and only

Free Spirit

a Shar Pei puppy, I discovered, has more wrinkles than the average Sarasota male, single or otherwise.

He was definitely too small for a frog's legs feast, even if it does taste like chicken. He wouldn't fill a cavity in my tooth let alone my stomach. He would barely be one tiny mouthful and I wasn't about to check around to see if he had relatives living nearby.

The third choice was my best one. I would get him out. Immediately I went into action. I grabbed my pride-and-joy, hand-woven with my very own two little hands, basket and threw it over him. On my gray ceramic tile floor I inched the basket, with my potential Prince Charming under it, to the door. I opened the door, lifted the front of the basket and gave the back a little shove. I watched as Mr. Leap Frog jumped sideways into the main part of my hallway.

He panicked.

I panicked.

He jumped into my bookcase and I trapped him there with the help of an extra ceramic tile. "Now what?" I thought.

It was still early in the morning so I went for a walk through the streets of my condominium area in the hopes of seeing a real live male who would remove my unwanted and unwelcomed house guest. "Let him get the warts," I thought.

No luck! I still had the problem. There were few male neighbors around and certainly no one I cared to tell that I was currently sharing my condominium with another and that "other" was not paying his fair share of the rent.

I went home and checked the bookcase. The poor little guy sat quivering in the corner. I replaced the ceramic tile and went to the community pool for a swim. I hoped that I would find someone who found my problem amusing and would offer to help.

111

Joei Carlton Hossack

The longer I waited, the more embarrassed I became about asking anyone. Now that I had seen him several times I realized that he was such a tiny creature. He was neither poisonous, nor aggressive and with pale green skin and a slender body he was not really offensive in appearance or habits. He definitely had more to fear from me than I did from him. My decision was made. I walked home purposefully, prepared to resolve the situation by myself.

I donned rubber gloves, dressed and armed to do battle. I covered the rubber gloves with a plastic bag. I opened the front door wide, removed the ceramic tile and peered in. He was either sound asleep, or possibly in a coma, wedged into the corner of my pale blue bookcase. I surrounded him with the plastic bag and scooped him up into my soft fist where he immediately sprang to life. With hearts, his and mine, pounding, I raced out the door, slamming it behind me. I opened my hand and watched as he took one small step for man and one giant leap for froggiekind.

I sincerely hope that I didn't miss my last chance of wooing and winning my Prince Charming!

I Was Not Supposed to Be Here Alone

Florida was to be our hideaway from the torturous weather of the north. My husband, Paul and I would winter in the sunshine, playing golf, swimming, hiking, biking and volunteering. Perhaps we would spend a day or two working each week at something we enjoyed. I could teach knitting or a class in needlepoint and Paul could work at a golf course or help a carpenter or assist in renovating our condo, anything to work with his hands.

It had been a ten-year dream to semi-retire in warmer climes.

We took six months finding the perfect hideaway and slowly moved in our belongings. We took extra time to put everything in its place. We moved in and stayed two days. It was May and getting hot in Florida. We sealed the condo and left to go traveling. We returned to Canada to visit friends and family and then back to continue our travels in Europe.

Our dream turned into a nightmare. In the blink of an eye my life went from riding high to the depths of widowhood. A heart attack while jogging in a German campground had taken my husband in the prime of life.

Not only did I have to contend with widowhood, but it was in a place with no family and only a few newly acquired friends in Sarasota, Florida. In the years that have passed I have discovered many things:

Happy or not the years go by very quickly.
I can travel alone.
I hate staying home.
I love getting up at five in the morning and writing.
I make friends easily.

Joei Carlton Hossack

I think I've lost my kitchen.

I love camping and sightseeing and movies and plays and opera and dancing and television and golf and, after many long years, I tolerate Florida. I do not like it. I was not supposed to be here alone.

1. Show Me the Way to the Womanatee Please
2. The Witness
3. Mobile House of Horrors
4. The Old Jewish Quarter of Prague
5. I'm On the Left, Right
6. Fly-By-Night
7. Christmas Confusion
8. The Last Frontier

The Single Years

Show Me the Way to the Womanatee Please

Occasionally I feel the need to air my gripes. You see I am a world traveler. At least I have seen enough of the world to think that I know what I'm talking about when I say that certain things really frustrate me and to make matters worse it is usually for some stupid reason.

The sights, sounds and smells of the British Isles, most of Europe, parts of Asia and Africa are all heartwarming and relatively familiar to me. I have walked the streets of towns and villages and large metropolitan cities and hiked the countryside of so many countries of the world that I sometimes think that there can be nothing new for me to see. Yet when I come across a sight that takes my breath away or makes my heart skip a beat I am always wonderfully surprised to realize that I have seen only a handful of sights.

I have never found language to be much of a problem either although I speak only English, a smattering of French and can understand a word or two of German. I frequently use the universal language of hand gestures and it gets me by nicely.

Foreign foods and drink conjure up marvelous memories for me. I drool over the thought of English fish and chips wrapped in the daily news. I long for my favorite French wine, Elsweicker, a combination of whatever is left over in the bottom of several barrels. Greek mousaka is a symphony to my palate and to sit down to a table covered with mini-bites of Turkish mezes plastered onto freshly baked bread would make my mouth water.

The only thing I have found the same universally was the necessity of using the bathroom, john, loo, lavatory, etc. in each and every country that I have ever been in. Although the

Joei Carlton Hossack

facilities have not always been up to my standards I have always known which one I was supposed to use. With the help of the word and a diagram I have always guessed correctly.....until I came home.....to America.

Each door, I feel, should have either 'men' or 'women' on it along with a little identifying picture. I can abide by 'guys' and 'gals' and don't have much of a problem with 'guys' and 'dolls', as I have seen so often. I even suffered through 'dude' and 'dudette' in various parts of the country. 'Bucks' and 'does', 'Tarzan' and 'Jane', 'buoys' and 'gulls' and a bunch of others have given me just a moment of doubt. Fortunately I am a dog lover and can tell instantly the difference between a 'pointer' and a 'setter'.

Florida.....now we are talking about another world.....and a strange one at that. I actually had to look closely at the pictures and try to figure out what was different about the two turtles on the door. I suddenly realized that the men's room door had a turtle wearing a tiny black bow tie while the ladies' room turtle had on high heels and a flower in her hat.

Since I spend several months each year in Florida I figured out the difference between doors labeled Manatee and Womanatee, because in Florida we know what a manatee is. Will a guest from a foreign country have any idea what the heck is behind door number one and door number two? I don't think so.

The piece de resistance, however, was at a small seaside restaurant called the Salty Dog, adjacent to the boat club, in Sarasota. The washrooms were a separate building and there I stood, in dire straits, shifting from one leg to the other trying to figure out if I am an 'inboard' or an 'outboard.'

Really, for the sake of necessity, can we be cute and creative elsewhere please?

The Witness

I was coming to the end of my morning constitutional and approaching an old wooden house that was badly in need of painting. A large, leafless oak tree filled with air plants and strangled by Spanish moss sat on one side of the property. Concrete blocks and decaying wooden boards hugged the side of the house. Except for a cracked driveway, an unkempt lawn surrounded the house, giving it an eerie vacant look. Something moved. I froze, rooted to the spot that threatened to engulf me in horror. I was the only witness.

I stared in fascinated horror as a snowy egret grabbed a snake in its beak, holding and squeezing it momentarily. In the blink of an eye the serpent coiled its body around the bird's bill and the snake was released with a little toss of the bird's head. The bird retrieved its prize over and over. Each time it was tossed higher and eventually it slammed into the ground. The bird moved and darted and attacked, careful to avoid the head and fangs of the snake in its struggle for life and freedom.

I stared. Each time the two-foot long reptile was picked up it became less and less aggressive. The great egret held its ground, keeping the snake in its beak longer and longer, squeezing tighter and tighter. The snake became less prone to movement. Gradually it no longer made any attempt to wind and twist. It just hung there, writhing slowly in the dance of death.

Even before death had claimed its victim the egret started to swallow, inch by inch, pausing in between sections. I watched as the entire snake slowly disappeared. I watched as the neck of the egret bulged in spots and the bulges moved to accommodate the snake that was still showing signs of life even as it descended into hell.

My mind was reeling as I walked away. Am I being prepared for my trip to Southeast Asia where the food might be somewhat different from my usual menu?

Mobile House of Horrors

I am fortunate by nature to be one of those happy and robust individuals. I make an effort to eat properly. I try to exercise daily. If I have skipped a few hours of sleep at night I have no qualms about treating myself to an afternoon nap. As a matter of fact I enjoy an afternoon nap even if I have not skipped a few hours of sleep and have discovered in the last few years that it is a healthy way to live. I try to balance my life between work and play whenever possible with a little emphasis on play.

I find, however, that when I am in pain, it is usually, for some strange reason, self-inflicted. I am referring, of course, to that extra glass of red wine that produced a migraine headache so horrific that I spent the night on my hands and knees and my head in the toilet bowl. I have also been known to force that extra bit of speed during a walk-a-thon for charity that took me to sixteenth place from seventeenth place and caused shin splints so terrible that even the healing hands of Reiki did little to ease the pain. Three days later I was still walking, shall we say, delicately.

My self-inflicted torture continued well past middle age, and I certainly should have known better. I realized that I could so easily have gotten on a plane in London, England and landed in Prague, Czech Republic two hours later instead of tormenting my mind, body and spirit on a bus.

In the planning stage, my reason for doing this to myself seemed so simple and reasonable. I had four weeks to kill before I caught my flight from London back to Toronto, Canada. I wanted to visit a few places that I had not seen before and, most importantly, I wanted to be flexible about the return trip. With a bus the return portion of the ticket could be left open and the fee for booking that return trip would be nominal, or in some cases, nothing. I also felt that my friend and traveling companion, Jean Higgs, and myself had a better chance of meeting other people to explore with if we took a bus. Besides, the lady at the bus station lied.

We booked the trip at the bus station in Bath, an exciting and lively, tourist town close to Jean's home in Temple Cloud, just south of Bristol. We had trouble getting a reservation for any bus sooner than the following Monday. Since there were not two seats available on any coach during that entire weekend we felt that it would be an interesting way to travel. Since so many others had chosen the same route, we were sure that our plan was the correct one for our needs. The booking agent made the trip sound marvelous.

For twenty-four hours, we were told, we would be on a luxury coach. It seems that I heard the word "luxury" and missed the word "coach." Meals would be served on board along with snacks and sandwiches. Coffee, tea, milk and soft drinks could be purchased at anytime and English money would be accepted on board. We were also told that there would be toilet facilities on board as well. For me, this last bit was essential because as soon as I can't.....I must.

We booked our trip. I don't know what that booking agent was smoking at the time, but the trip she was on, and the one she had planned for us was nothing close to reality.

Before catching our bus at Victoria Station in downtown London, Jean and I had a five-hour motorhome ride. That trip was done in two stages. Jean's husband, Bill, insisted that he drive us to our bus.

The first leg of our adventure, from Temple Cloud to Swindon, took place the evening before. We stayed overnight with their daughter, Debra and her family, enjoying their hospitality. We relaxed and delighted in an evening of wine,

Free Spirit

lively conversation, a bit of television and ended a most enjoyable evening with a hot chocolate toddy before bedtime. While I occupied their guest room, Bill and Jean slept in their motorhome.

We awoke very early, around four-thirty, the following morning. Jean made us all a little breakfast and some coffee while Bill and I scurried around trying not to wake the entire household, dressing as quietly as we could. We left the house like a pack of thieves in the night into the typical British morning dampness. We drove into London while it was still dark and were relieved that only the last half-hour of driving was done in rush-hour traffic.

At Victoria Station we had no trouble finding the bus going to Prague. At first sight.....and second and third sights, I might add, I could not believe that I had committed myself, and my all-too-trusting friend, Jean, to this mobile house of horrors voluntarily.

The seats were as hard as pews. They did not recline at all and in true German tradition, the seat part of the chair was so short and hit so far up my thigh.....zat you vill sit up straight.

All instincts screamed, GET OUT OF HERE! SAVE YOURSELF! BUT, we had just spent five hours on two different days getting to this final decisive moment. I stifled my instincts with a cup of weak coffee. Jean and Bill stifled theirs with a cup of tea. We looked at each other, cursed, laughed and climbed aboard. We found some unoccupied seats at the back of the bus. We took them.

To add to our misery there was no food, no coffee, no tea and no soft drinks on board. In fact if we didn't bring it on board we didn't have it. Fortunately, thanks to Jean's camping experience we had enough food with us, junk and otherwise, to supply a starving army on maneuvers. Jean prepared the food because she felt it would cut down on expenses. We never

Joei Carlton Hossack

dreamed that the food we had with us would have to carry two ravenous tourists through four countries.

We missed our usual hourly coffee and tea breaks. To make matters worse, as if that were possible, the restaurants we stopped at would not change English coin and if we wanted coffee or tea or use their pay toilets we would have to change Sterling notes. In each case we would have to change at least a five-pound bank note into the currency of that country. Much to our annoyance the bus stopped often on our journey. We did not want to cash our hard-earned money in France or in Belgium or in Germany. We waited and would cash what we needed in the Czech Republic. It was a long, dry, thirsty trip.

True to booking agents word, however, there was a toilet on board that could be used only in case of an emergency. Emergency it would have to be since I don't know when it was last cleaned. It certainly had not been scrubbed anytime during the month that we were on board.

My friend Jean, much to my annoyance, has the ability to sleep anywhere, anytime including on a hanger in the closet if it became necessary. Not me. When I wasn't trying to make myself comfortable sitting on the seat or the floor or trying to lie on two seats or three seats or the floor or generally twisting or contorting my body in a shape that it had no possible way of contorting into, I was writing a nasty letter to the bus company. I ended the letter by complimenting them on their ability to train their personnel to tell atrocious lies with such a straight face.

Also, to add to our miseries, we left England in the rain. Since the majority of the passengers were English, the rain made them feel sorry to be leaving home. Unfortunately the stormy weather followed us through France and Belgium. Just about the time we could enjoy a little sightseeing the rain stopped, night fell and all the lights on the bus went out. Being

Free Spirit

a relatively experienced traveler I made every effort to go out with the lights.

We arrived in Prague at nine the following morning. Michael Jackson's concert had closed the evening before. That was when we discovered that it was due to his concert that every seat on anything that moved was sold out that previous weekend. I wondered if any of the hundred spires that Prague was famous for would still be standing.

"Oh my God," I said to Jean wrinkling up my nose, suddenly horrified at the realization that we still had the return portion of our bus ticket.

The Old Jewish Quarter of Prague

It rained again on our last day in Prague but somehow it seemed fitting to be rainy and drab on this day. Today my friend Jean Higgs and I visited the Old Jewish Quarter.

Our first stop was the Old-New Synagogue. This temple dates from the year 1270 or possibly 1280 AD. It stands on the original site and is Prague's oldest Gothic monument and one of the oldest and best-preserved synagogues in Europe. The massive stone construction helped it survive in the face of fires, floods and other natural disasters. It survived the pogroms. It is still used for prayer services by the remaining Jewish community.

It was Yom Kipper (The Day of Atonement) and the synagogue would be closing at two in the afternoon. It was Sunday, the twenty-second of September in the year 1996. It had been our plan to go through the synagogue first because of its early closing. When we looked at our block of tickets we realized that each of the different museums had a time stamp on it and we must go through this portion first or we would not be admitted at all.

We had waited in a long line and once inside I was resentful of the extra money we paid to visit the Old-New Synagogue. They had charged everyone an additional eight American dollars. It was our last day and we could have used the money elsewhere since our funds were running very low. The temple was so small and barren that at first sight it didn't seem worth it.

Before entering the main part of the temple we noticed a small enclosed blockhouse at the back and I asked another

Free Spirit

tourist if she knew what the house was used for. She opened a guidebook, found the proper page and explained that when additions or funding were needed for the synagogue the money was placed there for safekeeping.

"The Jews were also very heavily taxed," she explained, "and that money was kept there as well."

"Considering what it cost to get in here," I said, "we are still heavily taxed." Both she and my friend Jean chuckled a little louder than to themselves and I hoped that no one else heard my remark.

Inside the house of worship, even with so many people around, Jean and I decided that we wanted to "feel" the peace. We sat on the wooden benches that lined the sides of the synagogue and tried to meditate but found there were too many people milling around and we could not concentrate. We sat and looked around the room, taking it all in: the speaker's tribune with the interior divided into two naves, political and religious, the red banner with the Star of David, and the pointed hat which was given to the community for helping Ferdinand I defend it against the Swedes in the year 1648 AD. We spotted the slots in the windows for women to view the services but not to participate. And we watched all the people who milled around, our favorite thing to do as we traveled the country.

From the Old-New Synagogue we went to the Maislova Synagogue. Mordecai Maisel purchased the land in the year 1590 AD to build his own house of worship. In its time the Maislova Synagogue was the most revered shul (synagogue) in the community. Mr. & Mrs. Maisel donated many of the artifacts housed there. Like many other synagogues it was destroyed by fire and rebuilt more simply in 1691 AD. The temple's originator did not live to see the new place of worship. He died in 1601 AD.

Joei Carlton Hossack

From Maislova we walked around the corner to the Pinkas Synagogue, dedicated to the people of Czechoslovakia who died in the holocaust. The temple was void of artifacts and painted pure white, a symbol of mourning. The words heard in the background were spoke in whispers.

The name of each victim was inscribed on the walls. Seventy-seven thousand, two hundred and ninety-seven names, all printed perfectly. The family name was printed only once and the given names and dates followed. Wall after wall after wall. Name after name after name. Every letter was perfectly formed – the names, the dates they were born and the dates of their deportation to the death camp. A little plaque, hanging on a rope standing two feet away from the wall signified what city, town or village the victim came from. Their entire existence was printed in one small space on a wall. The experience was numbing.

While Jean shook her head and commented, over and over, whispering the birth dates of the children, my eyes went from name to name looking for mine. Only one name came close, but my family background is Rumanian.

The second floor was the same as the first. The third floor was the same as the first and second but everyone there was compelled to go on. We went…..even if it was just to say, "we know that you lived." We were simply paying our respects.

My flippancy from earlier in the day was gone. Jean and I walked the marble floor slowly and in silence. Tears filled our eyes. So many people. So very many people. For a few moments in the courtyard we talked and shared our feelings. I was not prepared for the horror or the emptiness that I felt.

From the Pinkas Synagogue we walked around the corner to the Old Jewish Cemetery. The original gravestones

Free Spirit

dated back to the thirteenth century while the last grave was dug in the year 1787. There seemed to be no order. It was one of the most unusual and macabre cemeteries I had ever seen. A surreal configuration of leaning, fallen and crammed-together gravestones combined to total twelve thousand stones above ground with up to sixty thousand graves, in as many as twelve layers, below ground. Some headstones were in urgent need of repair while others stood erect, visible and prominent.

Jean and I found the tombs of Maisel, the principle figure in building and renovating Jewish buildings and homes during the renaissance, and Rabbi Lowe, the most learned Talmudic scholar in Jewish history. There were many tourists around and I took the time to explain why little pebbles had been placed on some of the headstones.

"It is simply a sign of respect and remembrance," I explained. "Even when I visit the graves of my mother and father in a cemetery in Montreal, Canada I place a little pebble on their gravestone just to say I was there."

A few people in the group, including Jean and myself, picked up a few pebbles and placed them on the markers.

After leaving the cemetery we entered the adjacent building. It was the Jewish Museum building and the home of pictures. The pictures came from Terezin about an hour's drive north of Prague. Terezin was Hitler's model city. The Jews were evacuated from Prague and ghettoed there. They lived, worked, studied, painted, wrote and attended school there. This is where the rest of the world viewed its citizens. Once seen, they were sent to other concentration camps or executed at Terezin.

All the paintings, drawings, stories, poems and memorabilia were saved. Some paintings, bold and complex, were by adult artists. Some, simple and naïve, were drawn by Jewish children. The Old Jewish Quarter in Prague is the best preserved in the world. Hitler wanted it that way. This was to be "The Museum of an Extinct People."

Somehow it seemed fitting that it was raining in Prague on our last day. That evening Jean and I attended Yom Kipper services at the Spanish Temple in Prague.

The rain stopped.

I'm on the Left, Right

"Did you hear the latest news from the Department of Motor Vehicles?" the comedian asked, not waiting for an answer. "They've decided to put the license plates under the car so the pedestrian will have something to read while he's waiting for the ambulance."

That joke comes to mind every time I find myself in a country where jousting was a sport and they have extended that mentality to driving their cars and I foolishly contemplate stepping off the curb. I know which way I'm supposed to look and I do take special pains to look in that direction. Then, just to make sure I'm doing it right I check the traffic coming from the other way. Then, of course, because I'm nervous about the whole process and it is uncomfortable for me, I check back to the correct side for the British Isles. By the time I actually dare to make my move and step off the curb, night has fallen and it's so much easier to check for the headlights, assuming of course that the drivers have taken the trouble to turn them on.

The summer that stands out best in my mind is 1994. I had spent most of the winter in Sarasota, Florida, driving on the right, and bits and pieces of the early spring in Montreal and Toronto, also driving on the right. On the evening of the nineteenth of May I left Toronto's International Airport, flew uneventfully across the puddle, and arrived in London's Heathrow Airport the morning of the twentieth.

Before my first week in Britain was over I had picked up, tuned up, driven and advertised my motorhome for sale. All of this activity was done, of course, on the left. In no time at all I was back to being a pedestrian, my motorhome, affectionately called the Puddle Jumper, having been sold.

Joei Carlton Hossack

Then came three-and-a-half months of right-drive/left-drive hell. I was back to being a pedestrian and having to watch for traffic whose major job it was to confuse, annoy and literally scare the hell out of me. In those few short months, I went from Britain where they drive on the left, to Turkey where they drive on the right, to Rhodes, Greece where they drive on the right, to the Greek side of Cyprus where they drive on the left.

Are you with me so far?

That was just the half of it. From Cyprus where they drive on the left, I returned to Rhodes where they drive on the right, and back to Turkey where they drive on the right.

Look both ways but do keep up and please don't tailgate.

I still had to return home. I arrived back in England where they drive on the left, and then back to North America where they drive on the right.

Safe at home.

I have had terrifying nightmares that have been less stressful then that particular summer and occasionally, when I'm behind the wheel of my truck, I have to make a conscious effort to remember which side of the road I'm supposed to be on. I have to remember to keep that center line, dotted or single or double, on the driver's side.

Perhaps when I'm older and prefer armchair traveling, I'll switch the remote control from my right hand to my left just to remember the good old days.

By the way, did you hear about the Siamese twins who went to England because the other twin wanted to practice her driving skills?

Just remember to look both ways, whatever country you're in.

Fly-By-Night

I am a true fly-by-nighter. Oh, all my bills are paid and I have not left a string of broken hearts behind, if that is what comes to mind. My friends and relatives are not looking to string me up for misdeeds that I have perpetrated on them either. It is just that I am happiest when I am making travel plans and since the cheap, last minute flights seem to take place in the middle of the night, I am, in the truest sense of the word, a fly-by-nighter.

At the moment I am sitting in a friend's living room in Temple Cloud, England, twelve miles south of Bristol. Jean and Bill Higgs are helping me decide if I am going to Majorca and Ibiza or Budapest and Prague. I still have four weeks to kill before my return flight to Canada, money is burning a hole in my pocket and my feet are itching to walk new lands, a sure sign that a decision has to be made soon.

Only a few of my British friends know that I'm back on English soil. My Canadian friends think I'm still in Turkey. My family believes that I'm already in Budapest and Prague and my American friends think I am where I told them I was going, which is, of course, Southeast Asia. I'm not in the habit of confusing them on purpose. It just sort of happened.

When I left my home in Florida in April I had fully expected to go to Southeast Asia, however, I needed a week or two to take care of some unfinished business in Canada. Nothing big or unsavory, just business. Within a week of being there, I discovered that my unfinished business would take over two months. A mortgage that was supposed to be renewed and could be done at anytime was now going to be paid off. I had to wait for the closing date.

TRAPPED!

Joei Carlton Hossack

I certainly would not allow that time to be wasted. A book, that had been screaming in my head trying to get out, had to be put to paper. Two months later, fifteen chapters of *Everyone's Dream Everyone's Nightmare* had been computerized. The notes for that book were meant for reminiscing purposes only and writing a travel book without specific information was difficult, however, I plodded onward and the book was at least half complete in its first draft.

HORRORS!

While I struggled with that book another realization hit me. My incomplete notes on my trip to Turkey were also never meant for anything other than reminiscing since I was not writing at the time of my first trip. If travels through Turkey were going to be a full-length book, I had better do it now while everything was relatively fresh in my mind. Where better to write a book about Turkey than in that country?

Southeast Asia would have to wait.

REALITY!

When temperatures get to over a hundred and twenty degrees and stay there day after day after day the brain turns to mush. Each day of writing was a struggle…..but struggle I did. In the seven weeks that I stayed in Kaş, Turkey, dreaming of a holiday in Iceland, my short story became the first draft of my book called *A Million Miles from Home*. Rewrites, I felt, could be handled in more temperate climes and the day I put my pen down, I desperately wanted out.

That was the same day I learned that a tour company selling the cheap, last minute flights back to Britain had gone bankrupt. The following day I learned that a train did leave Istanbul every night for Hungary, one of the few European countries that I hadn't been to yet. I could wend my way quite easily from Kaş south to Antalya. From there I would have to be on an all-night bus going north to Istanbul. I would need to find

Free Spirit

accommodations for a night or two or three or four, arrange for a transit visa through Yugoslavia, luxuriate (and I'm sure I use that term loosely) for twenty-seven hours on the train and arrive in Budapest at one o'clock in the morning. It was all too much for my soggy brain to comprehend. I needed out and I needed out quickly.

RESCUED!

By hounding the travel agencies I learned that I could approach other tour companies directly and was given several phone numbers to try. In the end I purchased a ticket to Manchester, England and left on the first available flight.

I slowly made my way back to my safe haven in Temple Cloud, stopping to visit friends in Chester, England, Wrexham and then Welshpool, Wales.

Almost two weeks have gone by since my return to the British Isles and the second of those weeks has been spent haunting travel agencies. Budapest and Prague are looking deliciously tantalizing. Before I could finalize the booking, looking like the cat that got the cream, Jean said, "I've never been to Prague you know. I'm going with you."

Amazing that in so short a time I have created a monster. Another fly-by-nighter has emerged from her cocoon.

Christmas Confusion

Traveling is supposed to be a learning experience. It is supposed to broaden your horizons. It must open your mind to all possibilities and to all people. It should make a person feel secure in strange countries because all people are basically alike and kind-hearted. It is supposed to bring understanding and a certain amount of peace and contentment. Why, then, after so many years of being on the road for more months than I stay home each year, do I feel so totally confused when it comes to Christmas?

After traveling in my motorhome for several months last summer I graced North Pole, Alaska with my presence, if you'll pardon the pun. I have been told all my life that when Santa Claus is not delivering gifts to all the good little boys and girls on the night before Christmas, the tiny village of North Pole is where Santa and Mrs. Claus hang their hats, so to speak.

There Santa spends his day reading his list and checking it twice while the elves are busy in the factory making all the toys. It is Mrs. Claus's task to feed and take care of Santa, the elves and the reindeer and, of course, to pick up after each one of them. This has been her job since time immemorial.

My excitement was high when I arrived at Santa's village. Since there were not many people in line, after all it was only August, I decided that it was important for me to get a candy cane from the jolly, fat man himself. I waited my turn.

He greeted me warmly, as Santa would, and asked my name. I told him my name and added that I had been good all year long, perhaps more by circumstances than by choice, but I was good and "I would like a candy cane," I said.

Free Spirit

He patted his lap. "Oh, no," I said with a chuckle, "I'm much to big for that."

He insisted that he could not give me a candy cane unless I sat on his lap. "Okay but don't blame me," I warned, "if you end up with a hernia."

How could I refuse Santa Claus? Besides, there it was, within my grasp.....a beautiful, red-and-white striped candy cane.

I treasured my prize. I had a candy cane given to me by Santa himself and nothing could have been more delicious. So where's the confusion, you ask?

This year's travels took me to a different part of the world. There I was, revisiting a part of the world that I loved.....Kaş, Turkey. I had been there about two weeks when a friend asked, "Have you seen where Santa Claus comes from?"

"Certainly," I said, "I met Santa last year in North Pole, Alaska."

"No, no, no," Michael retorted, "the real Santa Claus."

I was stunned. "What do you mean the REAL Santa Claus?"

"The real Santa Claus," Michael informed me, "was born in Patara, Turkey."

I shook my head at him. Poor, demented soul, I thought. Patara, Turkey, indeed. "I've been to Patara," I said. "I saw no evidence of Santa Claus. All I saw were very impressive archaeological ruins and an amazingly sandy beach with few tourists."

"Santa Claus was born there," he said. "His fame, however, did not spread until he became the Bishop of Demre," Michael went on to explain.

Michael was so serious, I just had to see for myself. A couple of days later we hopped on a bus heading for Demre and

Joei Carlton Hossack

Myra. In one hour and fifteen minutes we were in the thriving village of Demre. At the bus stop there were signs pointing to the Church of St. Nicholas ("Noel Baba" in Turkish). We sauntered over to the church. Although the church had been restored and offered a rare chance to see what a fifth-century Byzantine church looked like, this still did not prove that this was the home of Santa Claus.

We visited the church gardens. Lo and behold, there it was.....a huge statue, blackened with age, but surrounded by children standing in the center of the garden..... Mr. Santa Claus, himself.

"This," said my well-informed friend, "is where the legend of Father Christmas began in the fourth-century."

The guidebook that I always kept on me came in handy on this day and I read the story. *Father Nicholas was a Christian bishop who gave anonymous gifts to village girls who had no dowry. He dropped bags of coins down the chimney of their houses and the 'gift from heaven' would allow them to find husbands and to marry.*

"This is perhaps why he is the patron saint of virgins," Michael explained.

I continued with my guidebook. *Noel Baba went on to add sailors, children, pawnbrokers and Holy Russia to his flock. As his fame grew so did his parish. The people from the Roman city of Myra (named for the aromatic plant gum, myrrh) was added to his congregation.*

Since Myra was just a thirty-minute walk from Demre we went to have a look and stayed for the rest of the day. We climbed the rock-hewn tombs and walked the Roman theater looking over the barren countryside from several angles

It turned into a fascinating day of exploration and learning, but if he is the REAL Santa Claus then where is my candy cane?

The Last Frontier

I did it! I wanted to shout from the rooftops that I did it.

When I started on my incredible journey, I had just purchased what I hoped was a gently used, navy blue, VW Westphalia van and was sure that I wanted to keep it in pristine condition. I would wash it regularly. I would vacuum out the interior so the carpeting would stay fresh and colorful. I would keep the waxed finish free from mud, road dust and even water spots if necessary. I certainly would not consider plastering my home-on-wheels with unsightly slogans and bumper stickers. I changed my mind.

After risking life and limb, I completed seven weeks of traveling, not only the Alaska Highway but the Richardson Highway to Chitina, the George Parks Highway from Anchorage to Fairbanks, the Glenn Highway from Tok to Anchorage, the Haines Highway from Haines to Haines Junction, Yukon Territory and the Klondike Highway from Skagway, Alaska back to the Alaska Highway. I also traveled the Seward, the Sterling, the Tagish, the dreaded Taylor, with its twenty-three miles of mud instead of a road, and last but not least, the most intimidating road of them all, the Top of the World Highway. I now feel that I would love to plaster every visible inch of my vehicle with signs that say, "I did it!"

For those few foolhardy individuals who have braved traveling in the land of The Last Frontier, as their license plates indicate, you already know the thrill of it. For those who have not, I must dig down to the bottom of my toes for the courage to describe it. I don't ever remember feeling so insignificant and diminutive than as I did in the land of the midnight sun, where everything was so vast and awe-inspiring and where each and

Joei Carlton Hossack

every person living in that state can cavort on over one square mile of land without seeing another human.

The Alaska Highway starts in Dawson Creek, British Columbia and for me getting there was a feat in itself, since I started on my adventurous route in Sarasota, Florida. A giant marker in the center of the street on the main road in downtown Dawson Creek indicates the beginning of the Alaska Highway. This is milepost "0" and despite what the post says, the end of the Alaska Highway, according to the official certificate issued to me, is Delta Junction at milepost 1,422. Don't tell that to the people of Fairbanks who think the road ends in their fair city.

Dawson Creek is a small, homey community. The downtown portion is an easy walking town with only one main street and a country store/museum portraying life at the start of the Alaska Highway. A pioneer village takes up a few acres at the opposite end of town and well worth a quick visit.

Shown daily, or possibly hourly, at the museum is a feature film depicting the construction of the Alaska Highway in its entirety, or so they would like you to believe. I know better now but I watched the film with intense interest hoping to see the highway fully completed. The U.S. government started construction of the highway in 1942 and used it as a means of getting supplies to the soldiers stationed at bases in Alaska, since one of the battles of WWII was fought in the Aleutian Islands. I'm sure that the road may be completed sometime, perhaps even during my lifetime, but it still has a long way to go.

In Dawson Creek, thanks to an advertisement in the yellow pages of the local telephone book, my van was outfitted at one of the campgrounds with a metal and mesh screen to guard against rocks and bugs and to protect the headlights. When I finally got on the road heading north I was feeling rather confident.

Free Spirit

The people I had met in the campground were in camping vehicles of every size, descriptions and configuration. When referring to the Alaska Highway they spoke either in awe of it or with a tremendous amount of trepidation because, like myself, they had not started their journey yet.

We were all talking excitedly, yet apprehensively, about going "up" the highway. We had all heard horror stories about dozens of flat tires, broken windshields, broken axles or getting bogged down in mud deep enough to cover your wheels before coming "down" the highway. Either way we shared our previous camping experiences, our thoughts, hopes and a few of the fears that lingered in the dark recesses of our imaginations, especially mine.

Since many men had expressed their concern about my traveling alone, a couple of them invited me to tag along behind although their wives glared in disapproval. I decided against it. It was still a relief to see so many intrepid souls heading north. In my heart I knew that if anything should go amiss, campers were resourceful, caring individuals who would not leave a gray-haired woman, traveling alone, stranded by the side of the road. Before the trip was over, I learned that it was illegal to leave a person or motorist, gray-haired or not, stranded by the side of the road without stopping to help.

With bravado only on the outside, I left Dawson Creek the following morning and passed Fort St. John on my way northward. I camped that night in Fort Nelson. I was relieved, once again, to see a crowded campground and that most were heading north into the wilderness. There were many people to share our experiences of the road. When another van exactly like mine pulled in beside me, I found myself sharing a wonderful evening as well.

Pete, Joanne and I exchanged an abbreviated version of our life history, some travel experiences, some similar problems

Joei Carlton Hossack

with the vans we owned, and a couple of bottles of wine during and after dinner. The following morning we each had our fair share of a gigantic headache and hangover. Fortunately we did not have far to drive the next day. We ended up in different campgrounds but both camping spots were at Liard Hot Springs. Liard Hot Springs consisted of one hotel with adjacent camping spots, where I stayed, and a State Park campground where Pete and Joanne stayed. We nodded to each other as we passed on the path, each of us wearing a bathing suit with a towel draped over our shoulders.

Since hot tubs and natural hot springs are a special passion of mine, I could not resist soaking for hours, letting the mineral water wash over me and cleanse my body and my mind and revive my wine-soaked spirit.

Feeling much better after the dead-to-the-world soak, a well-earned, short nap in my camper and a light dinner, I spent several hours that evening wandering the same marshy area in the hopes of seeing an elusive moose that frequented the area.

Everyone I came across was in a small group or with a companion and I felt a little lost. I wandered alone for a short time and only after I returned to my camper did I realize that it was after eleven o'clock in the evening. I went to sleep that night, for the first time, while it was still light outside.

Since the campground was a short walk from the hot springs, I returned the next morning for another dose of relaxation and by the time I got onto the highway I was prepared for anything.....or so I thought.

It did not take long that morning to run into my first bit of construction and gravel. The truck drivers did not live by the same rules that other drivers do. While the passenger cars, campers, motorhomes and vans did their best to go slowly, stay as far to the right as possible and even show courtesy, a few approaching truckers did not and within minutes on this gravel

Free Spirit

road I knew my windshield would need replacing. Three different trucks heading towards me had been traveling so fast that the rocks, spinning out from under their wheels, smashed into my windshield. They hit with bullet force, shattering not only my windshield but my nerves and confidence as well. I cringed each time a vehicle came too close or seemed to be traveling too fast while coming towards me.

I was relieved when I finally reached Whitehorse in Canada's Yukon Territory. Some confidence returned and I began to look upon it as a magical, although somewhat intimidating, land.

I had entered a world that most people only see in pictures or read about in travel guides or view as an armchair traveler on television. Some mortgage their home for a week or two on a cruise ship to see the Inside Passage of Alaska. If they are lucky they fly to Anchorage and then drive to Denali National Park and possibly Fairbanks. Others let someone else do the driving and choose one of the many bus tours to Homer or Seward or Valdez. But not me! I had driven my own motorhome, by myself, from the west coast of Florida to Whitehorse, camping all the way.

In the seven weeks that I traveled the region I discovered not only a land where the sun never sets, but also mountain peaks so high they look down at the clouds majestically and are never without a crown of snow. I have walked on glaciers, touched icebergs, saw waterfalls cascading down from the heavens and watched ice worms wriggling about, knowing that a touch from my finger would incinerate them.

I have talked with people who have a pioneer spirit that rivals those of the Klondike Gold Rush. I have been where moose, caribou, bear and lynx still cause traffic jams and where dogs are not only man's best friend but their only link to the

Joei Carlton Hossack

outside world in winter. Perhaps I have even set foot where no other human has set foot.

I have a certificate with my name on it and the date I completed driving the Alaska Highway that I will display in a prominent place so anyone seeing it will know that I am not an ordinary mortal and that I have driven the highways of hell and survived.

I now feel, for brief moments in time, that I too may have acquired a bit of that pioneer spirit that is so prevalent in The Last Frontier.

My time here is at a close. It is the end of August and I am told that winter can come at any time and I do not want to be trapped in the north country. I have witnessed vastness beyond my wildest imagination. I have an incredible story to tell but my journey is only half complete.

I must leave and head for home.

1. A Long Day's Journey into Muck
2. Be Safe – Be Legal
3. Another Bad Hair Day
4. Carousel
5. Chased by a Storm
6. The Freedom Trail
7. The Agony of De-feet
8. The Light Bulb
9. Gardendale
10. My Kingdom for a Big Mac
11. An Inch Away from Disaster
12. The Heart of a Scoundrel
13. There's Something About Florida...
14. The Devil's Dilemma
15. Kansas Storm
16. Holiday Blues
17. Life in a Cocoon
18. A Fine Bit of Madness
19. Snow
20. Spare Tire Blues
21. The Power of the Battery
22. Port Aransas
23. Friends Along the Way
24. Life at the Flying J
25. Chian Singles' Group

Life On The Road

A Long Day's Journey into Muck

It had been a long torturous night. Most of the campgrounds on my northern route march had not yet opened for the season. After leaving the Escapee Campground in Raccoon Valley, Tennessee, I spent the first night at a Flying J in Walton, Kentucky. I had driven all day in a battering rainstorm and was spending my second night without hook up facilities at another Flying J in Beaver Dam, Ohio. This particular Flying J had separate areas for truckers and campers who wished to spend the night. There were just a few recreational vehicles parked so I left a space on either side of my camper.

I treated myself to a Flying J dinner off the menu rather than the buffet because the buffet didn't look the least bit appealing. The fried chicken looked greasier than usual, the ham steak was streaked with fat, the roast beef was too pink for my liking and everything else appeared to have been luncheon leftovers. Unfortunately the hamburger wasn't much better and took much too long to get to the table.

I watched television in the truckers' lounge for a couple of hours and was back at my camper by ten, prepared for bed. I was exhausted and fell asleep quickly.

I awoke several times thinking "when is that guy going to turn off his generator." It was morning when I discovered that it wasn't a generator. Some inconsiderate truck driver had squeezed his monstrous transport truck between a large fifth-wheel trailer and my little pisser and kept his motor running all night. The nonstop growl of his diesel motor kept the entire row of campers in their motorhomes, fifth-wheels and trailers awake most of the night. There wasn't one person the next morning who would not have gladly put this driver out of OUR misery.

I picked up some freshly brewed decaf in the restaurant, filled my tank with diesel and was on the road early. I stopped at my storage unit in Ypsilanti, Michigan and loaded several boxes of my book, *Everyone's Dream Everyone's Nightmare*, into the back seat of my truck for delivery to my Canadian distributor. Even though I was exhausted, it was much too early to stop for the day and the thought of getting stuck in early Monday morning traffic around Detroit sent shivers up my spine. I pressed on and headed for the border.

Despite the fact that there was no one in line, it still took close to a half-hour to cross. Finding out that I was a writer, the border guard wanted to chat. And chat we did.....writing, restaurants, travel, safety tips.

In Windsor, Ontario I hoped to spot a Royal Bank to add to my fifteen dollars in Canadian pocket money. Not only did I not find a Royal Bank, I missed the turnoff to the only open nearby campground, a KOA just east of Windsor. I didn't feel like turning back. I kept going.

It was around two in the afternoon when I stopped for lunch at one of the few travel plazas on the highway and discovered that I had miscalculated and had over a hundred dollars in Canadian money tucked away in my rarely used purse. I took a few seconds to thank the angel that must have been sitting on my shoulder.

The drive on Highway 3, a two-lane road going through every small town complete with stop signs and traffic lights, seemed endless. It was around six in the evening when I arrived at a friend's house in Dunnville. We kissed, talked quickly for a half-hour and I was on my way. I knew I would definitely reach the campground in Niagara Falls before dark, my main concern.

Free Spirit

The campground was within spitting distance when I got caught at the Allenburg Bridge over the Welland Canal with its bridge up. With a long string of vehicles I waited as the long, flat cargo vessel chugged by.

I was exhausted and it was almost dark when I arrived at Scott's Trailer Park. The campground was basically under water from the recent rain and snowstorms. Too tired to back my camper into the spot allotted me, which looked dry from the path, I decided to drive across the field to pull in front ways. As soon as all four tires were off the pavement, I sunk like a stone. I got out to inspect and the muck swallowed my shoes, my socks and the little energy I had left.

I walked over to the office. The owner looked as exasperated as I did but promised to come out with a tractor. He hitched the back bumper of my truck under the camper and told me to keep my foot off the gas pedal. He pulled. Not an inch did I budge. He tried again. Nothing!

"I think you'll have to call the auto club," he said.

"Let's try one more time," I said.

He pulled. I stepped gently on the gas pedal with the truck in reverse and I could feel it move almost immediately. Within a couple of minutes I was back on pavement. I tried to back into a couple of spots but nothing worked. I parked on the pavement for the night, connected my electricity with the help of an extension cord that would have extended across Niagara Falls if necessary. I borrowed several hoses and connected the water. It was a long day's journey into muck. I was happy just to be parked. I think I'll stay put for awhile.

Be Safe – Be Legal

I guess being female, fifty-plus, gray-haired and a solo full-time RVer has its advantages. Not only do I find myself meeting thoughtful and caring people on the road and in campgrounds, I find them at border crossings. After a brief conversation about what I was taking across the border, other than my personal belongings, what I had purchased and what I would be leaving behind, the border guard asked what I carried in the way of protection from the unsavory characters that I might meet along the road.

Although I was tempted to give the guard, who was at least twenty years younger than myself and as cute as a button, a smile and a wink and tell him that my "protection of choice" was a condom, I refrained from showing off and said, "I carry nothing."

His suggestion was WD-40, the largest can available. "Insert the red plastic straw that comes with the can" he said, "and tape it into place. Keep it under the driver's seat. That plastic straw," he said, "will be accurate for up to ten feet. Don't feel one little squirt will do it. Empty the can in the attacker's face."

His suggestion may save your life or mine and, best yet, it is perfectly legal to bring this "weapon" into Canada.

I haven't tried using WD-40 for that purpose yet and hope I never have to but I'll certainly keep it handy. Before I arrived at the campground that evening, I purchased two cans. One can went into my truck and another went into my camper since it is a separate unit and cannot be reached from the driver's seat.

Another Bad Hair Day

Oh, not another 'bad hair day' story you're saying to yourself. Does this woman ever have good hair days? Let me assure you that from the age of twenty onward they have been (almost) all 'good hair days' therefore the few bad ones stand out vividly. Each one of the bad hair days turned into mini disasters because (a) they were always preceded by a haircut and (b) I had to endure them until my hair grew out.

Here's how the incident started at my favorite campground in Niagara Falls, Ontario. I was in the pool with a few other regulars and another woman, whom until that very moment had only said hello to me in passing, started a conversation. She was a little plumper than I, much shorter than I, a little older than I and had a French accent.

"Oh," she said, "your hair is the most beautiful I have seen. It is always so curly. Where do you get your perm?" she asked.

"No, there is no perm. This is my natural hair," I answered.

"Oh, Mon Dieu, (I'm not sure what it means but the French say it a lot) I would love to cut your hair," she cooed. "I have been a hairdresser for more than thirty-five years. I have studied for many years in France with a master of the trade. Your hair is so thick and beautiful. I would love to cut it."

I thanked her and said nothing more about it because I'm used to compliments about my hair. With every haircut I have ever received, the beautician has remarked about my hair. It is short, soft, very thick and curly, and since the color seems to suit me, I keep it in its natural gray. In over twenty-five years it has not been tinted, sprayed, permed or straightened, something I tried a few times in my teens and early twenties.

Joei Carlton Hossack

Before our swimming was over, I had heard at least a half dozen times that she had studied in France under the best masters and that she would love to cut my hair.

It was about a month later. My hair had grown a little too long on top and since she had studied in France under the best masters and would "love" to cut my hair AND she lived right there in the campground, what did I have to lose? After all, I said to myself over and over and over, "No one can give me a bad haircut."

The date for the cut was that day. The time was set for around one in the afternoon. I walked over and she had a chair set out in her front yard. A tray with everything she needed was to her right and everything within easy reach. "The birds love to build their nests with hair," she said, so my locks were cut and allowed to blow far and wide in the breeze.

She was cutting my hair dry and with a razor, something I had never had done before BUT she had studied in France with the masters, I told myself. It must be okay. I cannot believe that I didn't even put my hands up to my hair to check it. I let her continue.

When she was finally finished, I put my hands up to my hair to feel it. This did not feel right. She held up a mirror. This did not look good. I stared in the mirror. I could not believe what I was seeing. It was ME!

I didn't thank her and felt rude about it.....but I was horrified. I paid her without giving her a tip. I walked back to my camper. Fortunately I didn't run into anyone I knew en route. I would have been tempted to duck into the bushes to avoid the laughing and pointing. I prayed that when I washed my hair it would settle down and go back into my familiar curls.

In short, it didn't. The sides were much too short so each individual hair stuck straight out and although my ears are relatively small and flat against my head they showed in their

Free Spirit

entirety. Again something I was not used to. The top was left too long and since it had been cut with a razor it stuck straight up and was kinky. Even after washing, it remained the worst haircut I have ever had in my life.

Yes, I'm sure she studied in France with the best masters…..at Miss Fifi's House of Poodle. All I needed was a jeweled collar.

Carousel

Having been a tomboy most of my life, I don't remember ever enjoying a carousel as a child but to be fifty-something, gray-haired and going up and down on a wooden horsey brought back wonderful childish delights to memory.

Fellow campers, Liz and Dave Pace, and myself drove from Niagara Falls, Ontario, Canada to Port Dalhousie, just a few miles from where our rigs were parked at Scott's Trailer Park. A couple of local newspapers that I picked up on a regular basis had written that a Scottish Festival would be in full swing at the boat club and on the downtown streets of the community for those three days in August. Since Dave is an avid, semi-professional bagpiper, regaling fellow campers with a daily recital, we were enthusiastic about a lively day with caber tossing, pipe bands, highland dancing and perhaps a treat (and I use that term loosely) of haggis on a bun, something I had only sniffed at and rejected in Scotland. As we approached, we actually thought we heard the haunting sound of the bagpipes in the distance. We drove down a few side streets so we could see them in full marching action. Talk about a vivid imagination. The newspapers were wrong. The parking lot of the boat club was half-filled with parked cars. Patrons sat drinking coffee or eating ice cream at the outdoor cafés. Absolutely nothing out of the ordinary was going on.

The town of Port Dalhousie is a charmer, located on the banks of Lake Ontario. We stopped to check the few boats that were floating in the harbor. Since it was a warm, sunny day I'm sure others were out cruising the calm waters. We stopped for a foot-long hot dog and French fry lunch. We strolled down the

Free Spirit

walkway near the back of the parking lot and came across an 1890 merry-go-round. At five cents a ride how could we resist!

Dave paid for the three of us to ride and we each rushed to our favorite horse or lion or whatever other beasts were available. We were on the move before we realized that we had all chosen stationary horses and after a quick view we realized that every other animal was taken.

Being the last of the big-time spenders I plunked down the next fifteen cents and we waited for trusty steeds that would move up and down on a carved wooden pole for the next three and a half minutes. Twice around was enough for three adults sitting on wooden saddles perched on the back of wooden horses. I now have a fairly good idea why John Wayne walked the way he did.

On our return to Niagara Falls we stopped at several wineries for a bit of sampling, a little more suited to our elevated station and age in life. We immediately reverted back to childhood when I discovered that my friends had never tasted a McFlurry, an ice cream treat and my cure-all for whatever ails me, available at the local McDonald's restaurant.

We returned to the campground in time for a short afternoon nap, a shared barbecue dinner, an evening in front of a raging fire and toasted marshmallows.

Does life get any better than this?

Chased By A Storm

I should have known better!
There was a hole in the clouds the size of a football field and the sun was out and shining brilliantly. The winds had died down to just a whisper of a breeze trying to trick me into a false sense of security. The trick worked.
The camper had been loaded onto the truck the day before. Everything inside was packed away and secured in the cupboards with pillows to keep whatever was breakable from shifting. I was ready to go. The weather report was not usually wrong and I could see black, forbidding clouds all around me.
I should have known better!
It was around eight-thirty in the morning on a late October day when I pulled out of the campground in Niagara Falls, Ontario heading west. I hadn't even gone two miles when the rain started. Well, to be honest, it hadn't actually just started. It had been raining all along because parts of the roadway were already flooded and I just sort of drove into it and couldn't see a way out without turning around.
At Lundy's Lane and Highway 58 I had to detour north to Highway 406 because the Allenburg Bridge, spanning the portion of the Welland Canal that I needed to cross, had sort of collapsed on top of a freighter months earlier and had been closed ever since.
The 58 led to the 406 where I had to slow down almost to a crawl. The rain pummeled my windshield in little splats giving me the impression that it was almost cold enough to freeze. I tried not to panic. The wind, at close to gale force, battered me around like a ping pong ball. I had gone less than ten miles and every instinct told me to turn around and go back to the safety and security of the campground. If I followed my

Free Spirit

gut instinct, I would be trapped for a week or more. The weather reports for the last several days indicated that the snow was coming. North Dakota and Minnesota had already been blanketed with twelve inches or more and the snowstorm was heading east.

    I wanted out. I kept going.

    Thirty miles down the road the rain stopped. The winds picked up. With both hands clutching the steering wheel for dear life, I drove west on Highway 3.

    I stopped for lunch. I stopped for a mini-break because my hands were hurting from clutching the steering wheel. I stopped at a supermarket to pick up a gallon of bottled water just in case I couldn't find an open campground and had to park in someone's yard.

    I worried that there would be a long lineup of trucks at the border and I would be forced to stay in Detroit. That didn't happen. I was ushered through quickly after a few questions and a cursory glance at my passport. It was later than I wanted it to be when I crossed the border from Windsor but I was delighted that the predicted snowstorm hadn't started yet. I stopped at my storage unit in Ypsilanti to pick up several boxes of books that I had left there. I decided to head down Highway 23 because Interstate 275 to Highway 75 south of Detroit had numerous accidents that everyone was blaming on the winds.

    I didn't think it was possible, but the winds got stronger as I headed south or perhaps it was just that my hands were stiff and sore and tired from the constant struggle. More than once, my truck and camper were blown into another lane with an unexpected gust and every truck that passed pulled me along in its wake. I kept going.

    The storm that battered North Dakota and Minnesota was now doing damage in the Upper Peninsula of Michigan and was expected to hit Detroit later that same day. I was glad to be

Joei Carlton Hossack

through there. I arrived in Toledo around rush hour and again slowed down to a crawl. So did everyone else. Even at a full stop my truck and camper rocked from side to side.

Then I did something that I rarely do. I drove until after dark. I pulled into the Flying J in Beaver Dam, Ohio a little after seven. I had driven four hundred and two miles and it had taken me over ten hours. I wanted to kiss the ground but I'm sure that if I bent down, I would have needed help getting up.

I settled in. I turned on my propane so I could start my generator. I turned on the television set and made a cup of hot chocolate. I didn't bother turning on the refrigerator. It was as cold inside as it was outside. The wind howled. I grabbed my purse and went into the restaurant for dinner. The place was crowded with truckers. It was warm and cozy and inviting aromas filled the air. I found a table, sat down and decided on the buffet because I was starving and the food was ready. It felt good to sit without moving but I found myself swaying unconsciously. During dinner there were three power failures, each one lasting just a few seconds. The waitress said that it had been happening all day.

I fell asleep before ten. The wind battered my camper and all the vents that were on hinges opened and slammed all night long. I awoke for the final time around seven. The snow was just beginning. I had to get out of there. While I prepared my camper for the road, I heated up some water for another mug of hot chocolate.

The snow amounted to nothing. The wind persisted. My hands and fingers ached. South of Cincinnati, the wind lessened to something almost tolerable. At five that day, and with another three hundred miles on the odometer, I pulled into the Escapee Park in Raccoon Valley, Tennessee about fifteen miles north of Knoxville.

Free Spirit

I connected my water, electricity and cable. I put a few things away and went into the clubhouse for a little chitchatting. It had been two long days of constant driving and I felt the need to communicate. There was a small group and we talked for about half an hour. Dinner was a microwaved baked potato with butter and grated cheese. I remember putting the plate into the sink and crawling into bed. That's all I remember. I'm sure my head hit the pillow but I don't remember when.

The Freedom Trail

Having been to the Niagara region so many times I felt that I had seen it all: the Falls, of course, the Floral Clock, the Butterfly Conservatory and the Minolta Tower. I had visited the Falls at night and had marveled at the cascading water dancing in the colored lights. I had also climbed to the top of Brock's monument on more than one occasion. I strolled the length and breadth of one of the most charming towns in North America, Niagara-On-The-Lake, and had sampled the wares at several wineries along the route.

It was, however, a small advertisement on a sheet with discount coupons given to me at the campground office that produced a day of adventure, a colorful history lesson and an immediate friendship with a local tour guide, Norma Tull.

I called the number listed to see if I could pick up the information for a self-guided tour beginning in Fort Erie, Ontario and traveling to Niagara-On-The-Lake, the end of the Freedom Trail via the Underground Railroad.

We were on the telephone just a couple of minutes when Norma offered to deliver the packet to me at the campground. Within a few minutes of face-to-face conversation with this soft-spoken, enthusiastic and knowledgeable woman, she invited me to watch a video with the Pennsylvania tour group the following day. It would be shown at the Nathaniel Dett B.M.E. Church (and the Norval Johnson Heritage Library). The United States claim Nathaniel Dett as their own but he was born in Canada. I gratefully accepted Norma's invitation.

Although the video was of some interest, the people around me, all African-Americans, were of major interest. I watched their eyes as the trials and tribulations of their

Free Spirit

ancestors unfolded before them. Unlike some fictional account of the events, this was drama in real life and touched the heart of each person watching. Before she left with the tour group, Norma apologized for not having room on the bus and invited to take me on a personally guided tour of the region at some time in the future.

It was several weeks before our days off coincided. She picked me up at the campground on a sunny but cool morning in late September and we discussed our plans over coffee and muffins at a local Tim Horton's Donut Shop.

When she pulled off the Queen Elizabeth Highway (QEW) one kilometer (welcome to Canada) east of Bowen Road, I thought something was wrong, but this was the start of my black history lesson.

She pointed to an open field adjacent to the highway. "That entire area was heavily wooded in the early 1800's and referred to as Little Africa. At all times, in the 1830's, the forest was home to approximately five hundred runaway slaves. This was where they experienced freedom, something they had never known before. It was also where they would learn to become self-sufficient. Most learned a trade, that of cutting and selling wood for the ship building trade, and each vowed to own property, again not available to them in the United States."

It was a short drive off Bowen Road where we visited St. John's Church. The residents of Little Africa were not welcomed here until 1880. The Coloured Cemetery was almost directly across the street from the church and a short way down one of the side roads. There were not many people buried there but we did check each headstone. Time had obliterated almost all of the information.

We drove to the Niagara River, the designated crossing for the freedom seekers. It was sign posted with a "Running Man" landmark. It is located directly across from Buffalo, New

Joei Carlton Hossack

York, the northernmost station on the Underground Railroad System. Each slave who made it that far arrived wearing a new pair of shoes, provided by a Rochester businessman, so his or her journey could continue a little more comfortably.

The source of the Niagara River is open-ended beginning in Lake Erie and ending in Lake Ontario. Those slaves unfortunate enough to miss the window of opportunity to land their rowboats safely in Canada's Fort Erie were swept down the raging river. If they did not drown en route they plummeted to their death over Niagara Falls. Those slaves who made it put their freedom and their lives in the hands of strangers.

For those who made it across the river, the safe house of Bertie Hall waited. A tunnel used by the Underground Railroad for smuggling slaves into the basement of the house was sealed when one of the sons of the Forsyth Family drowned in the tunnel. The history in the basement is in sharp contrast to the rest of the house. Bertie Hall is currently the home of Mildred M. Mahoney Silver Jubilee Dolls' House Gallery and contains one hundred and forty miniature houses in a collection that dates from 1780 to 1980.

From Fort Erie, with a stop for lunch, we toured sights a little more familiar to me. We drove to Niagara-On-The-Lake, stopping at Brock's monument, passing the Butterfly Conservatory, the Floral Clock and several wineries before stopping at the Cemetery for Butler's Raiders and their descendants. Col. John Butler defected from U.S. Fort Niagara, New York to Fort George on the British side, leading a black military battalion. We did not leave the area without paying our respects to probably the greatest "conductor" on the Underground Railroad, Harriet Ross Tubman.

It was fascinating that the history of one group of people was so interwoven with the history of two countries.

The Agony of De-feet

There are twenty-six bones in the human foot. It is absolutely amazing how much it hurts to break just one of them. Even one of the teeny-tiny ones located on the side of the foot.

I pulled into a Good Sam campground in Gananoque, Ontario after having driven farther than I had intended to on a hot, muggy day in August. I paid for one night, which was how long I planned on staying. I was on my way to visit my family in Montreal whom I had not seen in a couple of years. I pulled into my spot for the night. I connected my electricity. I immediately turned on my refrigerator since it was about ninety-five degrees and I always shut off the propane while I'm driving, hence no refrigerator, and went back outside with my water hose. While returning from connecting my water hose, half my foot found the ridge that ran alongside my camper. Half my foot did not.

I closed my eyes and sucked in my breath slowly so I wouldn't scream. I stood there for a second hoping the pain would subside. I limped over to the picnic table and watched as a large, blue egg developed on the outside of my left foot. I hobbled up the one stair before entering my camper and retrieved an ice pack that somehow had remained frozen. It didn't work. I limped over to the office.

I had to wait in line while the young girl behind the counter finished checking in a couple from Alberta. From the look on my face she knew I was in some kind of trouble and came out to see my problem. Without conversation I was lead back into the office. She sat me down and put a ten-pound bag of ice against my swollen foot. I gradually stopped whimpering as the pain subsided. I looked at my foot every few minutes. When it was frozen solid, it felt a whole lot better.

"Do you want to go to the hospital?" she asked giving me a puppy-dog look.

"It can't be broken," I said. "I wouldn't be able to walk on it if it were broken."

"Do you want to go to the hospital?" she asked again.

"Will someone be able to take me and bring me back?" I asked, not having a clue as to how far the hospital was or where or even in which direction. The fact that it would soon be dark bothered me. I knew I could find my way there, wherever there was, but I would surely get lost trying to find my way back.

"I'll call Rose," she said and before I could really make up my mind, she made the call. "Can you wait about ten minutes?" she asked. "They are in the middle of dinner."

Within minutes the door to the office opened and neatly dressed, freshly coifed, lipsticked Rose poked her head into the office to see what probably appeared to her to be a geriatric ragamuffin. My eyes were burning red, fighting off the tears. My T-shirt clung to me from the high heat and humidity and the sweat of pain. My sandals lay in a mini-heap beside a bag of crushed ice that should have been used for a margarita or a frozen daiquiri.

"Ready to go?" she asked.

"Could you drive me back to my camper so I can get my purse? I really don't know if I should be going," I answered. "Doesn't feel too bad now."

"Better to be safe than sorry. Let's go anyway," she said. "It'll ease your mind."

Without the ice keeping my foot frozen, I watched it swell again even though it had never really subsided. "Doesn't hurt much," I volunteered as I slowly wiggled my toes while sitting in the car. "I'm sure it's not broken."

Free Spirit

The hospital in Brockville, Ontario was thirty-five miles away. (The hospital in Kingston would have been the exact same distance but in the opposite direction) Rose knew exactly where it was since she has lived in the area all her life. She dropped me off at "Emergency" and went to park the car. I hobbled in. It was after seven and the sun was just starting to set.

I told the receptionist my story. She filled out the necessary paperwork. Rose returned and we waited.

It seemed to take forever. A nurse finally came and got me with a wheelchair. I was wheeled into X-rays and chided myself because I knew it couldn't be broken and I was wasting everyone's time.

I wanted to scream each time that the technician moved my foot to various positions to take X-rays. When that bit of torture was over I was returned to the hallway where Rose waited patiently.

"You haven't eaten yet," she said. "Would you like me to go get you something?" she asked.

"No thanks" I answered, "perhaps when this is over we can grab a sandwich nearby. I'm so sorry about wasting your time," I said. "They're probably going to slap on an Ace bandage and send me home," I said.

Another hour went by before Rose and I found ourselves in one of the examining rooms. We chitchatted. Nurses came in and went out. "The doctor will be in shortly to read your X-ray," I was told by one. One nurse came in with a bucket of water and strips of funny-looking cloth on a silver cart. My immediate thought was that they were using the room for storage. Talk about living in Fantasyland!

One of the orderlies, with whom I had been joking during the evening, arrived and advised me that I was getting an "ass-kicking cast."

Joei Carlton Hossack

"Yours is going to be the first one I kick," I announced.
"Are you telling me that it's broken?" I asked in disbelief.
"You'll have to wait for the doctor," he said. "I'm not allowed to tell you."

Well, to make a long story short, it was broken. To cast or not to cast was left up to me. With a heavy heat wave and an air conditioner on the fritz, I chose "no cast." It was one of those little bones that will heal with or without a cast but I would have to be "really, really careful," the doctor advised.

I got my Ace bandage and a prescription for Naprosyn, a painkiller with an anti-inflammatory. Rose walked the many blocks to where the car was parked and returned to pick me up at the door. She offered to wheel me outside in the wheelchair but I limped out under my own steam. It was now after nine-thirty and we had to find an open drugstore. Thankfully, Rose knew exactly where one might be open. She waited the twenty minutes inside the pharmacy for the prescription to be filled. We stopped at Tim Horton's Donut Shop for a bite to eat. I was starving but still in pain. I took a pill.

We arrived back at the campground just as they were closing the gate at eleven. Rose's husband was waiting for us along with several staff members and a couple of resident campers. Rose and her husband helped me into my camper. I didn't lock the door that night just in case I needed assistance and couldn't get to the door fast enough. I slept like the dead. When the sun came up I opened my door.

Rose came by the early next morning to see if there was anything I needed. She also explained that the owners and managers of the campground and especially her husband had been worried.....not so much about me but about her. They had sent this trusting, gentle lady off with a total stranger. I could have been some maniac. I could have been some deviate with mayhem on my mind. As each hour passed they became more

Free Spirit

and more concerned and for a split second thought they might call the hospital.....or the police.

I stayed in the campground another day. I thanked Rose with an autographed copy of my book *Everyone's Dream Everyone's Nightmare* and a cashable bookmark that would replace the gas she used getting me to and from the hospital.

A thousand blessings on Rosemary Burgess. It is because of people like Rose that many of us feel safe traveling solo around Canada and the United States. I don't know what I would have done without her.

The Light Bulb

It went out with a pop. I removed the bulb and discovered that the metal contact at the bottom of the bulb was flattened, like a mini-explosion had occurred. I tried a new bulb. It didn't work. It wasn't just the bulb that was finished. The fixture was gone. I would have to replace it. Fortunately I had another one since I felt one of the other fixtures was about to go in my Elkhorn Truck Camper. I wasn't in the mood to mess with it so I just left it. I secretly hoped that The Good Fairy would come along and change the fixture for me.

By late afternoon I knew that I had to do something because it was the only light that illuminated the kitchen and it would be difficult preparing even the quick-and-easy stuff that I ate with only the light from the stove. Around four in the afternoon I started pulling it apart, not knowing what I would find since I had never seen the innards of a light fixture.

I took the new light switch out of the box. It looked simple enough. There were only two wires, one black and one white. I decided to tackle the problem. I removed the four screws that held it in place underneath the large corner cupboard. I pulled the wires out from the hole and immediately started fiddling with it.

Getting the protective caps off was a different matter. I pulled and tried to unscrew it and pulled some more. After much effort and all the muscle I could muster, the white wires finally came undone. The black ones wouldn't budge. I went for the pliers and pulled and unscrewed and pulled some more. Nothing worked. I knew that I would have to cut off the cap. I had no choice. Whether I liked it or not I had to leave it since I didn't own a wire cutter.

Free Spirit

I fixed dinner to the bulb of the stove. It left lots to be desired but it worked. It was around seven-thirty when my friend Donna picked me up to go out for coffee. I was home around ten and flicked the switch on the fluorescent light in the center of the camper. Nothing! I turned the dual light on over the dining area. Nothing! Damn! I was not aware that when I blew the light over the sink, I blew all the lights in my house.

I was delighted to see that the refrigerator was still on electric and the time still glowed on the microwave, even though nothing else worked in the microwave. I groped in the dark for the remote and turned on the television set. I couldn't believe that I hadn't turned any of the lights on since early morning. I watched television in the dark. Out of force of habit I flipped on the light over my bed. Glory Be. It worked. How was that possible? Puzzling over what had happened, it came to me in a flash. I had blown a fuse. I had never done that before either.

The next morning I found the fuse box, opened it to see what I needed, and went out to purchase them. I bought packages in ten and fifteen strength and arrived home, ready to do battle.

I once again pulled, unscrewed and pulled again. It didn't work. A young man was walking past my camper and I called to him. I explained my problem. He said he had wire cutters and returned to his camper to retrieve them.

"I'll do it for you," he offered.

"Thank you," I said, "but I think I'd like to tackle this project myself. I've never done it before."

"Would you like me to turn off the power?" he asked.

"No," I answered. "I blew the fuse. You can just stand there and watch. If I electrocute myself you can tell them where to find the body."

Joei Carlton Hossack

"This is great," said Mark enthusiastically. "I've never seen a woman use a wire cutter. I'm very impressed."

I cut the protective end off. I gathered the white wires and secured them with a cap. I attached the black wire to the green wire and secured them with another protective cap. Mark suggested I cover the end with black electrical tape. "I'll go get some," he offered.

"Is it the same as hockey tape?" I asked. When he answered "yes" I said I had some in my toolbox and retrieved the roll from the back seat of my truck. I carefully wrapped all the wires, stuck them back up into the ceiling and replaced all the screws.

I thanked Mark and he went home. His camper was parked spitting distance from mine and I was glad of it. I wasn't finished yet.

I tried to remove the fuse but my fingertips weren't strong enough to grip it properly. I returned to Mark, apologized for being such a pain in the ass and asked if he had something that would remove a fuse. He brought long-nose pliers. The first fuse I extracted looked okay. The second one was blown. I replaced it.

I turned on all the lights. They all worked. I was elated.

"I cannot tell you how proud I am of myself," I said to my helper. "It is wonderful knowing that I can do it." In that split second I was hit with a mini-bout of depression. "How awful it is to know that I have to do it myself."

That is the plight of being solo.

Gardendale

This visit was a far different one from the first. I knew exactly what I would find, or at least, I hoped I knew.
I had found this particular campground in Gardendale, Alabama, twelve miles north of Birmingham, on my first trip heading south pulling a fifth-wheel trailer from Niagara Falls, Ontario to Sarasota, Florida back in November of 1998. Other than a KOA, it was the only campground listed in my *Trailer Life Directory* in or around the city. It was close to Interstate 65.
I followed the directions in the camping guide. I pulled in, didn't like what I saw, was sure that I was in the wrong campground since the sign at the entrance said Palomino, and pulled back out onto the side road. I ended up in a shopping center parking lot just a few miles away. I called the number listed and the woman on the phone gave me explicit directions, which included street names and landmarks. The directions led me back to the Palomino. I was too embarrassed to pull out a second time since several people had seen me the first time. Reluctantly I stayed.
The spots were too close together. They were not level. The road around the campground was potholed and washed out in places. I paid for one night.
That evening I met the owners Barney and Martha Booth. I also met Martha's sister, Louise Gable. To make a long story short and sweet, I stayed a week. I did four book signings in Birmingham and each evening had to give a full report of the people I met in the store, to the group at the campground who listened to each and every word and were as excited as I was at each sale.

Joei Carlton Hossack

When I tried to leave the day after the last signing, the entire family insisted that I stay. I could not spend Thanksgiving alone or with strangers in some other campground. I was invited to Louise's home to feast with friends, family and neighbors. That was my first trip.

On the way north from Florida to Canada, five months later, there was no question as to where I would stay. I was delighted to meet up with my friends again and enjoy their warm hospitality.

There have been many pleasurable trips to Gardendale since, but on my last trip, Martha picked me up around ten in the morning. I was given the royal tour of Louise's new home and then Martha and Barney's new home. They live only a block apart.

That afternoon I used Martha's phone to call the Compaq hotline since my new computer "crashed" and I needed to get it working. While I listened to recordings about Press 1 if.....or Press 2 if not.....for over an hour, a sumptuous lunch was prepared. During lunch Martha and I yakked like old friends.

We watched two movies and in my usual fashion fell asleep on their most comfortable couch sometime during the middle of each movie. I always woke up in time to catch the last half-hour. I luxuriated in a bathtub, my first in close to a year. I checked my e-mail on their computer.

Louise arrived from work around three and by six o'clock hands were held around the table while a prayer was said to thank God for the gift of good food that had been simmering all day, good health and friendships.

At eight-thirty that night Louise drove me home. I don't remember the last time I felt so relaxed. My overnight stay has now turned into five days.

Life on the road doesn't get any better than this.

My Kingdom for a Big Mac

My mouth waters when I think of one. The idea that it is complete in and of itself fascinates me. That it is all I ever really needed. It fills and satisfies and when I am ready for more, it is ready for me. So why didn't I buy it? Why, indeed. Where was my Big Mac when I needed it?

Instead of a Macintosh laptop, that I have enjoyed so much in the past and that did all I needed, why did I decide to switch to a Compaq Presario 1692? Unlike my Mac, this computer came equipped with a six-gigabyte hard drive, sixty-four mgs of ram, a built-in modem and a color monitor, something that was pure luxury from my standpoint. I guess the only thing it didn't have was the guts to work properly.

The first crash occurred on Thursday, March 23rd, 2000. Oh, I won't compare it to the stock market crashes of 1929 or 1987. I won't even compare it to the crash that occurred on April 6, 1999 on Interstate 65 heading north, twenty miles south of Louisville, Kentucky. That was the day that someone driving a gold Buick Marquis didn't see the only other vehicle on the road and ran dead center into the back of me. The disaster totaled my home, a one-year-old fifth-wheel trailer, sent me for weeks of physiotherapy and provided a perfect ending for the book I was working on.

This crash occurred sitting at the dinette table in my truck camper that happened to be parked at the Escapee Park in Summerdale, Alabama. I had been working on my book, *Kiss This Florida, I'm Outta Here,* for several hours. I needed a break and switched from work to one of the built-in computer games called Free Cell. With five games under my belt, I closed the game and prepared to shut down the computer. I returned to start, shifted the cursor to shut down, pressed down to click off the machine and the message read: "A fatal error has occurred. Press any key to close application or press ctrl, alt, del to restart computer." I pressed a key. The screen went black and stayed that way.

I turned the machine back on. Nothing! I pressed a bunch of keys one at a time. Nothing! I removed the plug, then the battery. Nothing!

"Surely someone at the park will know what to do," I said to myself. I waited until the four o'clock Social Hour. I asked around for a computer expert and when I found one I explained the circumstances. He said he would come over around five.

Right on the five o'clock button there was a knock at my door. The dead-as-a-doorknob computer sat on the table. With the help of the Emergency Recovery Disk, that came with the computer and a reboot floppy disk he managed to get it going enough to figure out that there was nothing wrong with any of the systems. It just plain didn't work. Ornery you might call it. Hunk of junk is what I called it.

Two hours later my knight-in-shining-armor was hungry for his dinner. I was hungry for my dinner. Frustrated I turned off the machine and told him that I would be in Birmingham in a couple of days and I would call on the Best Buy in that city, since I had purchased it at the Best Buy in Tucson. He suggested that I call Compaq directly. "That's what their support line is for," he explained. I promised that I would do that.

Ah, yes, Birmingham. I called the support line, went through a list of solutions with the expert on the other end and, since he couldn't suggest anything else, Greg promised to send out Recovery Disks. They would arrive in three to five working days at the campground in Nashville, Tennessee, my next stop.

Free Spirit

Seven days later, when I arrived in Nashville the disks were not there. I was told that more Recovery Disks would be sent out with one-day service. I left Nashville three days later, sans disks.

I stopped at the Best Buy in Knoxville. After checking all the Recovery Disks that they had on hand, they had none for the Presario 1692.

At the campground in Raccoon Valley, seventeen miles north of Knoxville, I called back the support line and was advised by the manager that NEVER do they promise one-day service and if I did not clean up my language she would have no alternative but to hang up on me.....and, yes, she did understand my frustration. I'm sure she did NOT understand my frustration because working for Compaq almost guaranteed that she used a Mac, a Gateway or a Dell.

I told her that my next stop would be Niagara Falls, Ontario, Canada. She promptly issued a case number and transferred my call to the Canadian branch. I spoke with Jeff in their Ottawa Office. He was very nice, took down all the information and asked if I would mind waiting on the line while he checked to see if they could send out Recovery Disks to a campground in Niagara Falls. Need I go on.....my computer was purchased and registered in the States and there was nothing they could do.

I called the campground in Nashville and the owner promised to forward the disks to Canada as soon as they arrived. A week after my arrival in Canada, the disks arrived. I was delighted. I rebooted the machine. I used the CDs to reinstall all the programs.....the printer, Office 97, Publisher 98 and my digital camera. I blissfully went back to work on my book since it was in the final editing stages and I was well behind schedule. Faithfully I saved everything on several floppies.

Joei Carlton Hossack

Nearing the end, I edited twenty chapters in one long, tiring day. I needed just a few Free Cell games to end my day. I played games for about a half-hour. I closed off the game, clicked the cursor at start, shifted to turn off the machine and clicked off. Message read: "A fatal error has occurred. Press any key to close application or ctrl, alt, del to restart computer." I pressed any key and the machine went black taking with it twenty final edited chapters that in that one split second I had forgotten to save on floppy.

I called the Support Line. They issued a reference number but I would have to return the computer to the States.

I rebooted the machine and thankfully it came on. I worked ten hours straight one day and thirteen hours straight the second day, completing the final editing of my book, transferring everything onto several disks. I finished the book on Saturday.

On Sunday I packed up the machine and took it to Radio Shack in Niagara Falls, New York since that was Compaq's closest dealer. On Monday I packaged up two of the disks for the graphic designer in Alexander, North Carolina and four disks for the printer/binder in Nashville, Tennessee and then everything was mailed out.

Two weeks have gone by and it seems all is lost. The computer is floating around at the head office someplace in Texas and all the disks for my book *Kiss This Florida, I'm Outta Here* are either lost in the mail or stuck in customs.

And other than that Mrs. Lincoln how did you enjoy the play?

An Inch Away from Disaster

I had volunteered my services to a new, innovative RV company in exchange for a month of camping and the privilege of displaying, in their booth, the two travel books I had written at the world's largest gathering of "people on the move."

The Gem and Jewelry Show had recently ended and we were setting up for the RV show in Quartzsite, Arizona. Thousands of information packets had been assembled and boxed in the days preceding the big event. Deliveries of these packets, brochures, metal stands, computers and boxes of my books had to be made to the big tent. Bottled water along with a refrigerated holder for the water had to be picked up in the next town and set up at the booth. The work was backbreaking and endless and the show hadn't even started yet.

Even though my friends, who also happened to be my employer for the show, used their personal vehicle for all the running around that had to be done, I wanted the use of my truck. I wanted the feeling of independence whether I really needed it or not.

The entire procedure, from start to finish, normally took about ten minutes so I waited until the last minute to remove my Elkhorn truck camper from my Ford F-250 diesel truck. I unscrewed and removed the metal rods that held the camper securely into the bed of the truck. I had prearranged with the manager at the campground office to have four concrete blocks delivered to my site. One block was to be placed at each spindly leg that stabilized the camper on the truck and supported it off the truck. The concrete blocks were part of my standard procedure. I used them every time I removed my camper and I

Joei Carlton Hossack

removed my camper every time I was parked someplace longer than a day or two.

I jacked up the camper, unplugged the electricity from the truck bed and drove out from under. I started lowering the camper. I preferred the camper as low to the ground as possible since it felt more stable just a few inches off the ground with only room enough for the sewer hose connection. I lowered the two front legs to the count of five and proceeded to lower the back legs to the count of five, then going from front to back several times so as not to bend the camper frame.

A soft thud, a noise I had never heard before, stopped me dead in my tracks. I walked around the camper. To my horror, two of the concrete blocks, both on the same side of the camper, had cracked. The back one had broken away entirely. The front had split in two but stayed under the leg.

I was flustered for a split second. I knocked on the door of my neighbor's motorhome, explained my problem in short concise sentences and all three occupants came out to help. Lyle produced a box of large wooden blocks in various shapes and sizes. More people gathered around, most just curious. With everyone standing around I called on my angels, both living and spiritual, as I tend to do in a crisis. I needed all the help I could get.

All hands held onto the camper.....more for something to do than for actual muscle. With my heart pounding and my mind racing in all directions, desperately trying to ignore the fact that my only home could fall over at any second, I worked quickly. I inched it up as far as I dared, which wasn't far, and prayed that the block wouldn't crumble away any further. I backed the truck under the camper, with a clearance of about four inches, as far as I could go without raising the camper any higher. I lowered the camper onto the edge of the truck bed and

Free Spirit

watched as the weight of the off-center camper pulled the truck bed down. With the electric jack I raised the front leg.

Just as Lyle removed the concrete and shoved a large wooden block in its place, I heard a third concrete block crack. With the camper still sitting a few inches in the truck bed I raised the other front leg, which was the last one to crack, and Lyle supported that one with another wooden block.

I raised the camper off the truck on its new front blocks, evened up the front and back and another block of wood went under the back leg that had broken away completely.

My nerves had had more of a workout than I was prepared for that day. I jacked up the entire camper, backed my truck under it as it was supposed to be and there it sat for the two weeks of the RV show.

Home Depot here I come. I'll take four hardwood blocks to go please.

The Heart of a Scoundrel

I had decided to try an evening on the cheap, which is something I occasionally do in my full-time travels around America. I had reserved a camping spot in Rally Park at Lazy Days in Tampa, Florida for the seventh of the month. The Escapee Rally was to start on the eighth and I arrived on the sixth.

I pulled into a spot in front of Camping World, part of the Lazy Days complex, at around two in the afternoon. I walked over to the clubhouse at the RV Park and proceeded, with their computer, to check my e-mail. From my actions you can surmise that this was not my first visit to this particular camping facility.

By four o'clock I was back at my camper to relax and enjoy reading the rest of Susan Sloan's first novel, *Guilt By Association*. I had an early bite to eat and decided to walk around the grounds outside Camping World just to make sure that I wasn't alone. There were many motorhomes in that section of the lot but for my own peace of mind I needed to know that at least some of them were occupied.

I met Dorothy and Fred who were out 'de-watering' their thirteen-year-old black Lab. While Fred stayed to talk to the person, (whom I will refer to from now on as Mr. Scoundrel) who was unhitching his gold Cadillac from his thirty-four-foot Coachmen, Dorothy and I continued our walk. In touring the parking lot, we spotted the front view of his Coachmen.

The accident was obvious. The passenger side window was a spider web of cracks with bits and pieces that had fallen both inside and outside the motorhome. Splintered shards of

Free Spirit

fiberglass were all that was left of the front panel that covered the engine. The passenger side bumper area was gone.

"What happened?" I asked the owner, who was still trying to unhitch his car.

"Well," he said slowly, "I've owned this motorhome for about four months. For three of those months it has been in the shop for one repair or another. So there I was driving down the highway. This truck, with a company logo on it, is coming up fast and passing me on the inside lane. I could see the guy is on the phone. He really isn't paying attention. He hit the dirt a couple of times and I know, at some point, that he is going to lose control. He is just too reckless. He runs off onto the soft shoulder one last time, overcompensates, and comes straight back at me. I could have gotten out of his way, you know, " said Mr. Scoundrel.

"Are you here to have it repaired?" I asked innocently.

"No, I've told his company that they are paying for a new one. A motorhome that has been in an accident," he said, "never works right again."

Now there was a fact that I had to agree with since bits and pieces of my twenty-two-and-a-half-foot fifth-wheel trailer had been left on the I-65 heading north about twenty miles south of Louisville, Kentucky the previous year.

It was four days later when I ran into the same couple having breakfast. "Well," I asked, "did you find something you like?"

"Yup," he said, "sure did. It's a beauty. A gorgeous Class A, thirty-eight-foot long with a couple of slides," he said proudly. "The thing costs four hundred and fifty thousand dollars," he volunteered.

"Four hundred and fifty thousand dollars!" I said, not believing my ears. "What could possibly make a motorhome worth four hundred and fifty thousand dollars.

"Well, it's got this great full-sized microwave/convection oven," he said.

"Okay," I responded, "that brings us up to seventy-five bucks."

"We love the built-in washer and dryer which our last motorhome didn't have because it was too small."

"Okay," I said, "we're up to seven hundred and seventy-five dollars. What next?"

"It's a diesel pusher so the engine is in the back and real quiet."

"Okay, now you're talking," I said, "we're up to fifty thousand seven hundred and seventy five dollars."

Needless to say, by the time they left the breakfast table they were nowhere close to explaining the total cost of four hundred and fifty thousand dollars. He did mention that it was going to be great being able to park the motorhome next to their yacht when they wanted to sail or near their plane when they wanted to fly someplace special. That explained a lot and in my mind made the four hundred and fifty thousand dollars sound like pocket change.

I wished them good luck as they headed out and I stayed to finish my breakfast.

In walking back to my camper I ended up walking down the row they were parked on. Mr. Scoundrel was sitting outside on the back bumper of his Coachmen.

"Is this your new baby?" I asked, pointing to the motorhome parked beside his trade-in.

"Yup," he replied.

I walked around the outside of both his old and new rigs. "She's a beauty," I commented. That's when I noticed that his wife was sitting in their Cadillac. "Why aren't you inside moving things around?" I asked rather perplexed.

Free Spirit

"Well," he said, "when I put my key in the lock I heard something snap. Can't open the door. We're waiting for the repairman."

"Four hundred and fifty thousand dollars don't buy you much these days," I quipped. "Next time try buying something with a little quality to it."

I again wished them well and returned to my ten-foot Elkhorn truck camper where everything worked.

There's Something About Florida....

Something happens the minute you slip over the border into the flat, low-lying state. It doesn't just happen to you as you begin to hunch over and start shuffling from one place to another; it seems it happens to everything and everyone around you. In that split second everything ages, rusts or just plain falls apart. And it happens rapidly, making the most ungodly noises in its death throes.

I pulled into the Escapee Park in Zolfo Springs in central Florida in mid-afternoon. I was disappointed that there were no hook-up spots available but decided to stay for the rally called Cracker Capers. A Cracker, not to be confused with Fire Cracker that shows an immediate spark of life, I learned, was the original settler to that region.

A man in a golf cart escorted me to a spot in the boondock area. I parked, opened the propane valve, turned on the refrigerator and put a few things away, making myself as comfortable as possible without electricity. I went to the social hour in the clubhouse and met some of the other Escapee members. A few of the members looked somewhat familiar since I had been to several other Escapee parks and had attended numerous camping gatherings known as Escapades .

After a hectic and tiring day I went back to my rig early. I read for awhile and then tried to fall asleep. That's when I heard the cacophony.....roosters crowing. The noise hadn't bothered me during the day but without benefit of any other sounds, like my television or radio, it was like bedding down in a barn. I slept little. I tossed and turned a lot. I swore constantly. I dragged myself out of bed the next morning looking considerably older than when I had gotten into bed.

Free Spirit

Less than twenty-four hours later the refrigerator signal went from 'propane' to 'check'. Since I had a full tank of propane I suspected that the battery, less than two years old, must have been running low. I also knew that it shouldn't have been running low since it had been called to duty for only one day and usually ran three or four days without a problem. I switched on my generator and the refrigerator responded by switching to electric power. As long as the refrigerator was running, with a week's worth of perishables inside, I didn't worry. I shuffled off to meet my friends.

I returned about an hour later to discover that my propane alarm was heralding its existence. I manually switched it off. Ten minutes later it was blasting again. I opened all the vents, including the escape hatch over my bed, the back door and a couple of the windows. All was quiet. I left. When I returned the alarm had gone off again. My friend, Ann Cote, checked her manual. The propane alarm, according her manual, can be set off by a spray from an aerosol can. It will also rear its ugly head and sound the alarm for fuel, liquor or alcohol vapors.

"My alarm has gone off while rolling on deodorant, using hand cream and dabbing perfume behind my knees. As a matter of fact my alarm, as sensitive as the delicate fair-haired princess in *The Princess and the Pea*, has gone off while peeling an orange," she confessed. "That discovery was made after entering the state of Florida and buying a bag of the beauties for a dollar-fifty. Would you like me to disconnect the alarm?" questioned Ann.

"Yea, go for it," I said. "This is really a pain."

Down on her hands and knees she removed the screws that held the box to the wall and discovered that she couldn't disconnect it that way. "Why don't we cover it with a plastic bag?" she said and promptly wrapped the housing in plastic. Success!

It worked perfectly UNTIL we closed the door and started to walk away. We returned to the rig. "Why don't we remove the fuse?" she offered.

"Great," I said.

We found the fuse box. She tried to remove the fuse with her fingers but that didn't work. I then made the mistake of handing her a knife. Since we are both still here to talk about it and my rig did not burn to the ground with the sparking, we tried a different approach and got someone else involved. Lynn Brazelton, using his fingers to jiggle the fuse, was finally able to remove it. The light went out on the alarm. The propane continued to flow. The generator continued to work. I finally relaxed.

At ten that night I turned off the generator and let the battery, that was now fully charged, do its thing. Exhaustion finally took over and I fell asleep listening to the damn roosters.

I awoke at four in the morning. It was pitch black outside. The barking dogs had joined forces with the roosters and since I couldn't fight them I decided to stay awake (like I had a choice) and read for awhile. By five, while it was still dark outside, my eyes closed. I quickly nodded off.

"Beeeeeeep! Beeeeeeep! Beeeeeeep!"

Terrified, I bolted upright. Nothing! I must have been dreaming, I mumbled to myself. I lay back down.

"Beeeeeeep! Beeeeeeep! Beeeeeep!"

In sympathy for the propane alarm not being in working condition, my smoke alarm blasted out. I got out of bed, staggered over to the alarm located on the wall near my back door and twisted it off the wall. I removed the battery from the smoke alarm, slammed it down on the table and returned to my bed.

Free Spirit

There was now a symphony of barking dogs, crowing roosters and a cat fight......it sure sounded like a cat fight.

Tonight, so help me God, I'm going to rip the batteries out of those damn roosters. I'm going to hunt down those dogs and chain them to their owners and I'm going to fix one of my special delicacies called fricasseed feline for a midnight snack.

Sleep well. I'm sure everything will work properly the minute I leave Florida.

The Devil's Dilemma

"What are your favorite Christmas lights?" asked the interviewer of the older woman who was standing in the doorway waving.

"Oh that's easy," she answered looking rather haggard. "It's the bright red taillights of my children's car as they head down the driveway to their home taking the grandchildren with them."

That's exactly the way I felt when the Illinois State Good Sam camping rally was finally over. It was such a relief to see most of the big rigs heading out the gates for parts unknown and knowing that I was staying one extra day for a well deserved bit of rest and recreation.

* * * * *

I had driven the last hundred miles from Joliet to Henry in ninety-five degree weather and was looking forward to checking in, plugging in, turning on my air conditioner and hibernating for a couple of hours before making any attempt at being sociable on that Labor Day Weekend. Unfortunately that was not to be. I had 20-amp service, with three camping units sharing one electrical pole outlet, and the use of an air conditioner, microwave or toaster would blow the fuses, or so I was told. I made the mistake of telling the guide that I would unplug the electricity and turn on my generator so I could turn on my air conditioner.

"Oh no," he said. "If you want generator parking I'll have to park you someplace else. You paid for electricity. Where do you want to go?" he said in a tone that made me want to smack him.

Free Spirit

I stayed where he put me. I plugged in my electricity, turned on my refrigerator and opened all the windows and air vents. Fetid air, heavy with moisture, thanks to being parked next to the racetrack on the fairgrounds, seeped into my camper. I took one deep breath knowing that I couldn't stand more than a minute or two of being inside the camper. It felt like a sauna.

I locked the door behind me and went to the activity hut. The giant doors at the front and back were open. I sat at a picnic table directly under a ceiling fan hoping for even a whisper of moving air. The others parked at the table said nothing as I sat down and picked up a puzzle piece. Any spare energy was used for cooling rather than communicating.

It was a two-sided puzzle with the back side being exactly the same as the front side only turned ninety degrees. The words "The Devil's Dilemma" and "The World's Hardest Puzzle" were written on all sides of the box. We said nothing as we worked.

By the third day of agitated or little sleep, my nerves had come unglued. I had walked the fairgrounds on several occasions and listened to noisy air conditioners behind the locked doors of the camping elite (staff mostly and those needing oxygen) knowing that only a dog or cat was inside.

I finally got up the courage and pulled a no-no that my camping neighbors wholeheartedly supported since I was beet red, sweating profusely and looking like I might faint at any moment. I unplugged my 20-amp service, cranked up my generator and blasted my air conditioner. I fell asleep almost immediately and woke up refreshed. I exited two hours later singing my own rendition of "Let it snow! Let it snow! Let it snow!"

On the day of my lecture titled Solo World Travel I learned that they had overbooked the room. That was definitely a bad omen. They changed the day from Friday to Saturday.

Joei Carlton Hossack

The two-thirty time slot remained the same. My only saving grace was that I would be lecturing in the only air-conditioned building on the grounds. Despite the change, the room was packed. I'm sure everyone with 20-amp service and an urge to sleep was there.

Bill and Gail McCrabb, part of the electrical crew, came and listened to my lecture. They were so impressed with my travels and my bravery that they invited me to dinner at their rig. I sat with at least eight others, mostly crew members and their spouses, and feasted on a smorgasbord prepared by my new friends.

That was my last lonely minute spent with the good people of the State of Illinois Good Sam camping rally. We ate together the next evening as well, sharing our leftovers, before heading inside for the entertainment.

On the last morning of the four-day rally, the temperature plummeted to seventy-two degrees, which was heavenly, and that night it went down to forty-four degrees.

Hey guys, lighten up. I was just kidding about "Let it snow! Let it snow! Let it snow!"

Kansas Storm

I have no idea why Dorothy and Toto were so damned eager to get back to this place.

I'll be the first to admit that when I'm on a lecture or book signing schedule I just drive rather than take the time to do any sightseeing. On Interstate 70, however, there is really nothing to see except for the miles and miles of road that stretch ahead with the occasional billboard that reads "One Kansas farmer can feed 28 people AND you." Even my mother couldn't put me on that kind of a guilt trip and she too could read my mind.

My first overnight stop as I headed west was at a Flying J in Warrenton, Missouri. There was nothing dramatic to report but the news on television that night did mention that a couple of tornadoes had touched down in various parts of Kansas that were in direct line with the road I was on. My second night was at another Flying J three hundred and sixty miles from the first one in Salina, Kansas.

When the rain started I thought I was prepared. I wasn't. The four inches seemed to come at once and within minutes the parking lot was flooded. I was grateful to be on solid pavement instead of at a campground where the "green, green grass of home" would have turned into a murky lake trapping me in my camper as surely as the La Brea tar pits trapped the mastodon and saber tooth tiger.

The drizzle and fifty-mile-an-hour winds the next day kept me from going too far. I found the library in downtown Salina, one of the largest, most beautiful and best equipped, I had seen in awhile, and took an hour to answer my e-mail. When I got back onto Interstate 70, the rain and wind increased.

Joei Carlton Hossack

The other cars and trucks on the road with me never slowed down. Fifteen miles west of Salina I found a campground and pulled off the road. I plugged in and flipped on the television set to squint at either of the two fuzzy channels that were available. I turned it off, turned on my computer and went to work. I accomplished much. That night the wind howled like a pack of wolves, bending, snapping and crackling all the mature trees. I didn't sleep well.

I drove two hundred miles the next day in those same winds and watched my diesel fuel, at almost one dollar and seventy cents a gallon, evaporate as I struggled to keep the truck on the road. I seemed to be fighting a losing battle. At two-thirty in the afternoon I pulled into a campground in Colby, Kansas.

The "storm warning" system on television indicated that tornadoes had touched down in eastern Colorado and western Kansas. I didn't have to watch television to see what was heading my way. The biggest, blackest clouds whipped around directly overhead. The lightning lit up the sky and the thunder, clapping right above my flimsy, poorly insulated roof, was deafening. Golf ball-sized hail was predicted and the radio announcer advised that "with no warning whatsoever a tornado could touch down in your area. Be prepared to take shelter."

We were a small group in the campground. We went into the office to see what protection would be available to us if we suddenly found ourselves in the path of destruction.

"Not to worry," said the owner, "we have a storm cellar."

I should have known. After all, this was Kansas.

Miraculously, we were safe, although a tornado touched down less than five miles away and we could see the funnel cloud from where we were standing. And several more touched down within a couple of hundred mile radius.

Free Spirit

Dorothy, as long as you were with the wizard who could grant you your fondest wish why not ask to move to California?.....oh yes.....they have earthquakes. Why not ask for Florida?.....oh yes.....they have hurricanes. Why not go to the Dakotas?.....oh yes.....they have floods. Why not Arizona?.....oh yes.....they have dust storms.

Okay Dorothy.....you win.....maybe there is no place like home.

The next morning the sun came out. The wind died down. It was so beautiful, I decided to stay another day with Dan and Shirley Bourquin of Bourquin's RV Park. There might not be much to see in Kansas but the people were sure friendly.

Holiday Blues

Life on the road as a solo RVer can be tough at times. You get used to doing all the driving. The hitching up and unhitching becomes second nature, after a learning curve that causes big, blotchy hives to break out all over your body but, nevertheless, you learn. Cooking for one becomes a breeze as does doing the dishes.....but eating alone.....well, that does have its disadvantages. Cleaning fifteen or twenty (or even forty, but I can't see that ever happening to me) feet of RV living quarters is manageable, even with a couple of slideouts. Just about the time you get used to all of it, along comes a holiday like Thanksgiving and there is that momentary punch in the belly. Where's the family when you need them!

My own family is a little spread out. Both my brothers and both my nieces, the identical twin daughters of my brother Harry, live in Montreal, Canada. Brrrrrrrrrrrr! Definitely too cold for my liking. Besides they celebrate Thanksgiving in October. Well, to be honest, so did I. I happened to be camping, writing and lecturing in Niagara Falls, Ontario and was invited to the home of friends whom I had made at the Canadian Authors' Association meeting.

To continue about my family, I also have two nephews, the sons of my older brother Nathan, who live in British Columbia. Although it is a little milder in winter, I'm told that the rain and dreariness of the west coast can put one into a depression that only a couple of weeks in the sunny south would cure.

My sister and her two sons are in Southern California. Now that's what you call gorgeous weather but too far and so expensive. Speaking of far, I have one last nephew living and

Free Spirit

working (teaching English) in Korea. So I repeat, alone for Thanksgiving. Oh, woe is me! Life on the road as a solo RVer can be tough at times. At the end of October I left Niagara Falls and worked my way south and east. I lectured at a rally on Solo World Travel in Frederick, Maryland for the Good Sam Camping Club. I did book signings in most of the major bookstores in Nashville, Tennessee and Birmingham, Alabama, leaving family, friends and cold weather behind as I headed south. I drove the one hundred and ninety miles to the Gulf Shores, around Summerdale, Alabama, and pulled into the Rainbow Plantation Campground the day before the holiday. I set up my camper prepared to bide my time.

Life on the road as a solo RVer can be tough at times. I spent my second Thanksgiving having a turkey dinner feast with all the trimmings prepared by two hundred of my closest friends and acquaintances in a beautifully decorated clubhouse. I prepared a dish to share and did none of the cleanup.

Gotcha!

A week later I was still hanging around the Plantation. There was a four o'clock social hour where I could meet everyone who had arrived that day, many of whom I had met at other social hours in other parks associated with the Escapee Camping Club.

There was a Thursday night dinner at a Chinese Restaurant in Foley, about five miles south of Summerdale on Highway 59, with fifty or so fellow campers. I tasted spicy crawfish for the first time and thoroughly enjoyed the new flavor. There was a Sunday ice cream social, and, for me, nothing beats ice cream with chocolate sauce. There was a Saturday night soiree at a barn, a place that I will never find on my own. The country music with David Parker at the helm, along with six or seven other musicians, was fantastic and interrupted at nine so we could help ourselves to a buffet meal complete with fried chicken, roast beef and incredible brownies.

There were new friends to make or I could chitchat with old friends. There were puzzles to do, games to play, movies to watch, live music to listen to and, when time permitted, I did a little editing on my new book.

Life on the road as a solo RVer can be tough at times but somehow I seem to be managing.

I left the Plantation only after I received a call from my friends Amy and Norman Prestup. They would wait for me at a KOA in Lafayette, Louisiana. We had not camped side by side since we got caught in the first Gulf War together.....but that's another story.

Life in a Cocoon

I wish I had a couch that opened into a bed!
I wish I had a comfortable lounge chair!
I wish I had more storage!
I wish I had a separate shower!
I wish I had more counter space!
I wish I had a computer work station!
I need more room so my fire alarm won't go off every time I boil water for tea!

These are the woes of living in a truck camper. Twofootitis, the desire to have two more feet than you've got, hits the first day of camping of the very first trip. Twofootitis, I have discovered, hits everyone at some time or another, even those running around in a small city, as I like to refer to the motorhomes that dwarf my 'pisser.'

Would I trade in my ten-foot Elkhorn Truck Camper for something bigger with all or most of the amenities mentioned above? Well, yea, just make me an offer.

Actually, to be brutally honest, I'm not quite ready to change at the moment. You see my present home is a matter of choice. I've had the small motorhome, where everything had to go with me when I drove out for a carton of milk. I've pulled a fifth-wheel trailer that intimidated me every time I left the campground with it trailing behind. I never really got comfortable pulling it because I never had any lessons in hitching, unhitching, backing up or parking and always worried about being cut off on the highway or getting lost on some God forsaken back road and not being able to turn around.....all of which have happened.....and, of course, I did survive. I would probably still be pulling my fifth-wheel if I did not get rear-

Joei Carlton Hossack

ended at ten in the morning on a bright, clear day on Highway 65 and have my home totaled twenty-miles south of Louisville, Kentucky.

Without wanting the hassle of towing another vehicle, a truck camper is the only way to go. The back of my camper hangs two feet over the back bumper. That area houses my black and gray water tanks. My propane generator sits back there in its own private locked box. On the other side is a locked box for the sewer handles. I do keep both of those compartments locked…..one to prevent the theft of a valuable asset and the other to prevent mayhem most unsavory.

The inside seems to have more accessible cupboard space than my twenty-two-and-a-half-foot fifth-wheel trailer. The so-called bunk bed, located above the table, will accommodate someone weighing less than one hundred and fifty pounds. Fortunately I don't know anyone that weighs less than one hundred and fifty pounds so my sheets, towels, crock pot, binoculars, bits and pieces of personal stuff, camping equipment and my printer sit up there nicely when not in use.

I have equipped the only large storage compartment in this entire camper with four large plastic drawers, so that area has become moderately practical. I have used up, pared down, thrown out and put into a four-foot by four-foot by eight-foot storage unit things I no longer use regularly or often enough to keep on board. Slowly this camper is becoming my home.

I cook a lot. I clean a little. I work a lot. I entertain inside a little. I travel a lot. I see a lot. I meet a lot of people. I am enjoying my life a lot.

The best part of this camper is, even for something as small as this, the bed is always made up for sleeping. The camper itself can be very affordable. I can park it into any regular parking spot. A good heavy-duty truck handles it quite easily although I have equipped it with air springs over the back

Free Spirit

wheels. It is easy on fuel, a major consideration with skyrocketing diesel prices. When I'm in a campground longer than a couple of days, I unhook the metal rods, securing the camper into the bed of the truck, by hand. I jack up the camper with the electric jacks, unplug the electricity from the bed of the truck and drive out from under. I then press the buttons and the camper lowers itself. If it sounds simple, it is because it is simple. I can hook up the camper myself in about twenty minutes. If I have help it takes about an hour-and-a-half and the helper is a lot closer to being murdered than he will ever know.

So far there is nothing I haven't been able to do alone. Fortunately being solo, full-time and female, when I've asked for help, someone has always been around to lend a hand. All too often they are around to help when I have not asked.....I guess they just can't believe that I can back up straight for eight feet.

This is my home, home on the range.....or by a lake.....or in a campground.....or in a Wal-Mart parking lot.

A Fine Bit of Madness

Near the end of the film *Zorba the Greek*, Zorba dances by himself. His arms are spread out and his hands are open towards heaven. He shouts, "everybody needs a little madness." Well that's my story and I'm sticking to it.

I had just spent five days camping at a Good Sam Rally in Centreville, Michigan. Although the staff members were most welcoming, the participants warm and friendly and there were plenty of activities and lots of entertainment, the rally seemed endless. The temperature soared to over ninety-five degrees every day with a humidity index that pushed the temperature to above one hundred and five degrees before noon. To add to our misery, we were not permitted to use our air conditioners because of insufficient power at the fairgrounds. My camper became a mini-sauna. If horses sweat and men perspire and women glow.....then I became a Christmas tree in July.

It was our last morning. I had had my coffee and had said my good-byes to a few new acquaintances. I was waiting in a slow-moving line at one of the two dumping stations. During my hour-long wait, I fingered the contents of the plastic box that was propped on the hump in the center of my truck containing my CDs, maps, a couple of dollar-off coupons at various campgrounds, and lo and behold, a one-day pass to a nudist colony in Michigan. It had been sitting, gathering dust, for over a year.

Michigan is a big state. I decided to check it out on the map, just to kill some time. Union City, by all my calculations, looked about fifty miles away and in the direction that I was heading. I had one extra day before needing to be at my next

Free Spirit

appointment. Before modesty could take hold, my brain went into overdrive and all I could think about was diving into a cool, refreshing swimming pool.....naked.

Madness, I tell you. It was sheer madness. I have never done anything like this, nor have I really seriously contemplated doing anything like this. I called the campground and discovered that the pass was still good and "yes, I could camp there overnight." The drive was on back roads and since I suspected that they did NOT have billboards advertising their whereabouts, I called when I reached Union City and got specific directions. I was amazed at my calmness. I still believe, and will to my dying day, that my clamminess was due to the weather and not anxiety.

Not knowing what to expect, and knowing full well that I wouldn't run into anyone with whom I was even slightly acquainted, I felt I would probably go (largely) unnoticed as most over-fifty, gray-haired, bespectacled, (pleasingly) plump women do. After arriving and checking in, I was given (fully clothed by a fully clothed guide) a tour of the facilities. The volleyball court, an indoor swimming pool and hot tub, a lake with boats for rowing and fishing, a sandy beach and an outdoor conversation pool were first rate and very inviting.

For my first venture or should I say "adventure" I decided on the conversation pool.

(A) The first thing that struck me funny was that when I went to strip off my clothes in my camper I closed the blinds.

(B) Everyone who walked passed me on the path greeted me and smiled. They gave me the once-over like I was still twenty years old. This was done with a look and a smile. There was no ogling or leering or smirking, nothing that made me the least bit self-conscious. I, of course, did the same.....except that I did ogle, leer and smirk.

Joei Carlton Hossack

(C) In the conversation pool, I was immediately acknowledged and made comfortable enough to join into the conversation. I confessed that this was my first "nudist" experience and was admired for my bravery.

From the conversation pool, a group, myself included, went to the mud bath. Another first experience. Chivalry prevailed. A hand was extended so that I wouldn't slip. Conversation flowed as it had in the pool. We scrubbed and rinsed off in the lake and unfamiliar hands gently washed the mud from my back.

Exhausted from the sun and all the new experiences, I returned to my camper for a short nap but couldn't resist one phone call. My friend Bal in Boston likes to live vicariously through me and when she answered her phone I asked as nonchalantly as I could muster: "Doesn't the American Constitution guarantee that all men are created equal?"

"Yes," she said, recognizing my voice almost immediately. "Why do you ask?"

"Have they been sold a bill of goods," I responded with a giggle.

"Okay, where are you?" she asked.

We talked and laughed for the next half-hour before saying good-bye.

That afternoon in front of the wide-screen television set in the lounge I was approached by familiar faces.

"Hi," the couple said in unison, "had we known that you were a nudist we would have spoken to you about it at the camping rally this morning."

"This morning," I responded, "I wasn't a nudist." (So much for not running into anyone I know.)

That evening I danced, totally uninhibited, to music on the new jukebox with friends I had met in the pool.

Free Spirit

The experience, on a scale of one to ten, was easily a twelve. I am still an over-fifty, bespectacled, gray-haired, (pleasingly) plump woman who mostly goes unnoticed in a crowd. Thanks to the one day at Turtle Lake in Union City, Michigan I'm back to feeling the way I should.....feminine, beautiful and desirable. The toughest thing about my one day of madness occurred the next morning when I had to put my clothes back on and go out into the big, anonymous world.

Would I do it again? In a minute.....as soon as the sunburn stops stinging.

Snow

I couldn't believe my friends had wished this for me. I called every last one of them. They all denied it of course…..the nerve of them. They all must have prayed long and hard for me to have a white Christmas even way down south in Deming, New Mexico.

Early Christmas Eve morn I opened my blinds, as I started every morning on the road. The sky was dark and ominous. It looked like a sprinkling of rain as unheard droplets beaded up on my windows. Since it didn't seem all that cold with my windows and vents closed and my electric heater blasting away, I opened the door. I was stunned. They weren't raindrops at all. They were snowflakes. Surely they wouldn't last long…..not way down here on Highway 10 in southern New Mexico.

By noon the flakes had banded together, each one a force to be reckoned with. In outlying spots around the campground the snow accumulated in anthill-sized mounds. By three in the afternoon I knew that no one would believe me without proof in print. I started making snowballs from the frigid downy afghan that blanketed the hood of my truck. I made one small snowball, with hands and fingers that quickly resented the work, for each one of my jealous friends. I took pictures with my digital camera of the little pile of snowballs that looked like they were ready to be fired from a miniature cannon.

By five the snow again became flurries and just a hint remained when we all gathered in the clubhouse, forty or so people bearing beautifully wrapped gifts and a dish to share.

It was warm and cheery and noisy inside with everyone toasting the season with a warmed fruity punch or homemade

Free Spirit

eggnog. Without a chimney, Santa had to use the front door to make his entrance but was made to feel welcome when he finally arrived. I must have been good all year, not by choice I can assure you, because he had a gift for me in his large red sack that he had slung over his shoulder. The weather outside might have been frightful but Christmas at an Escapee Park in Deming, New Mexico was delightful.

Dear friends and family, I don't care what kind of weather you send my way. I'm not going back to Canada or anyplace north of Highway 10 in the wintertime. My destination is just over the next hill.

Spare Tire Blues

I don't know exactly when the problem started. I was on my way to a Good Sam camping rally in Fryeburg, Maine and stopped for groceries about eighteen miles from the fairgrounds. Before going into the store I walked around the truck and camper, as I always did, just to see if everything was intact. All the little doors and cubbyholes were closed. The rods that held the camper securely in the truck bed were tight and nothing was dripping from under the truck. I was just about to walk away when I spotted a bulge on the inside back tire. I was sure I had run over something unsavory like a small animal or an exceptionally large wad of bubble gum that was just about to pop. I went closer to inspect. It was certainly not bubble gum. As a matter of fact it was not anything that had once been alive. The bubble was in the tire. I panicked.

A gray-haired man in well-worn jeans and an old checkered work shirt was just getting out of his pickup truck. I asked him to check it out. He confirmed it. He gave me directions to a tire store on the route that I was headed. I left without the much-needed groceries.

I drove slowly and stopped at Cooper Tires. The balding, flabby-looking salesman behind the desk wouldn't even look at the truck with the camper on the back and since the tires weren't Cooper Tires, my problem didn't hold much interest for him. I continued on to the fairgrounds and was relieved when I made it without further incident.

The rally was fun and a big success, business-wise. On the Sunday, the last day of the rally, I disconnected the truck from the camper, called AAA, and they not only changed the tire but showed me that I did indeed have a jack and exactly where, under the hood, it was stored.

Free Spirit

Monday morning, after some running around and telephoning I found a Super Wal-Mart in Windham, Maine. I had purchased the current set of Goodyear tires at Wal-Mart in Coralville, Iowa twenty thousand miles before. I drove the sixty miles to Windham with the damaged tire roped into the bed of the truck.

I was delighted that the manager confirmed that there was a flaw in the tire and it could be replaced with the same brand name for the sum of one dollar.

I was sorry that I had watched the young man change the tire. He struggled to get the spare tire off. He struggled to get the new tire on and when he tried to jack up the truck he broke the jack handle so my truck was suspended in mid-air until knowledgeable help arrived. The manager went out and lifted the truck with a different jack, more suitable for a three-quarter ton truck.

"That kid has no idea what he's doing out there," I complained to the manager.

"Don't worry," he said, dismissing me like I had just escaped from a place where the name is whispered. "It'll be okay."

I watched as the kid struggled to put the spare tire back in the carrier located under the back end of the bed of the truck.

If that were the end of the story there would be nothing to write about. It wasn't.

* * * * *

It was Canadian Thanksgiving night and I was crossing the Skyway Bridge from St. Catharines to Niagara Falls, Ontario. It was dark. I was doing about fifty-five miles an hour and cars and trucks were whizzing by me like I was stuck in second gear. I had just passed the last possible exit off the three-lane bridge when I heard and felt the crash. Without

Joei Carlton Hossack

really knowing for sure, I knew in my heart what had happened. The spare tire had crashed down on the highway and since I slowed immediately to a crawl and pulled to the extreme right side of the bridge, I knew it was still dragging behind. I slowed to about two or three miles an hour and hugged the wall. If the tire was going to fall off completely, I wanted it to be on what little shoulder was available on the bridge. A car or truck hitting a truck tire, complete with rim, at sixty or seventy miles an hour would surely become airborne or roll over and someone would be seriously hurt or killed. I panicked. I called 911.

When I told the operator of my predicament she told me to keep driving. "Do not stop on the bridge," she warned. My call was transferred to the Ontario Provincial Police.

My mouth was almost too dry to talk. Again I explained my predicament and was again warned not to stop on the bridge. They were dispatching a patrol car.

Within minutes I saw the flashing lights behind me. I tried to pull over but the officer, through the bullhorn, told me to keep driving. I breathed a little easier knowing that if I lost the tire it would be retrieved safely.

As I approached the top of the bridge there was one patrol car in front and two behind. Still doing about three miles an hour I made it across the bridge and onto the soft shoulder following the lead patrol car. There was a grand reunion when we all stopped. The spare tire was still intact hanging onto the back of my truck. The tire was okay. All the bolts were there. The spare tire carrier was ruined. One of the officers crawled under the truck and removed all the bits and pieces. The hardware went into the truck and the tire went into the truck bed.

I produced my driver's license. A second officer took down all the pertinent information before following me to the first exit off the Queen Elizabeth Highway. He worried that I

Free Spirit

would lose the spare tire from the truck bed since I couldn't tie it down.

I was at the Ford dealer bright and early the next morning. After checking under the truck, the manager said that it looked like someone had tried to steal the tire and had loosened the bolts.

That was the dealer's theory. My theory was that the young man who changed the tire in Windham, Maine really didn't know what he was doing.

Care to venture a guess of your own?

I sent a letter to the manager at Wal-Mart in Windham, Maine and another to the head office in Arkansas. I'm still waiting for a reply. It's only been two years.

Where are you Sam Walton?

The Power of the Battery

Despite the long drive, most of it in through the Great Smoky Mountains, it had been a great day. That afternoon I had signed a new contract for the distribution of my second book *Everyone's Dream Everyone's Nightmare* with a North Carolina firm. I had returned to the Escapee Park, seventeen miles north of Knoxville, Tennessee in time for the four o'clock social hour and shared the good news with the rest of the campers. Several approached to congratulate me. One couple asked if they could buy my books and, of course, I had to let them know that I was down to my last thousand copies. Giving up a single copy would not even make a dent in my stock of books that was causing the back seat of my three-quarter ton diesel truck to heave.

After dinner I brought a copy of *Restless from the Start* and *Everyone's Dream Everyone's Nightmare* to their camper. While I autographed them to Bob and Dee Poole, Bob asked Dee when they had last put water in the battery.

The look on my face must have told them the entire story but I verbalized it anyway. "You have to put water in a battery?" I said, scrunching up my forehead like I had just been told some unbelievable fable. "I thought they were sealed units. I've never put water in mine."

"I'll help you check it tomorrow," said Bob knowing that it would be too dark within the next few minutes to check it that night.

They came by early the next morning with a screwdriver, a gallon of distilled water and a plastic cup so a stream of water could be poured exactly where it should go, if needed. I let Bob work his magic in removing the battery from

Free Spirit

its private little cubbyhole, prying off the dual rooftops and staring deep into its bowels. He had me stare down the hole as well. Even I could tell that the battery was bone dry. I could see the tops of every cell. I held the battery at an angle. He poured.....and poured.....and poured.

I promised I would check the battery every month and have been doing so faithfully ever since. I don't do much boondocking so the battery gets little practice other than phantom use, i.e. the propane detector, the electric starter on my hot water heater, the refrigerator and possibly a bunch of other things that I don't even know about.

It was at the International Good Sam Rally in Gillette, Wyoming where I ran into problems for the first time. Since electric power for the four days of the rally would run an additional one hundred dollars, due to the fact that the event was generator-powered, I chose to dry camp. I decided I would run my generator for about an hour a day around dinnertime to boost my battery.

The day started early. By eight in the morning I was having coffee with the singles' group. By nine I had to be at the booth that I shared with another author. Every evening I met the group of singles for dinner and after dinner I made sure that I was back on the grounds in time for the fabulous entertainment. I ran my generator for about an hour or less just before bedtime since without a daily dose of television I suffer from withdrawals.

On the fourth day I returned to my camper to grab some lunch before heading back to work. That's when I saw it. My refrigerator light read "check." I opened the refrigerator door to see if anything was amiss. I checked the propane to make sure I hadn't used the entire tank. It all looked okay. I turned off the refrigerator, then turned it back on. It went back on propane. It seemed to be working again. I left.

Joei Carlton Hossack

I returned a half-hour later to find the refrigerator back on "check." I repeated the procedure and again it worked. I went back to my booth. I explained the problem to Stephanie Bernhagen, the author of *Take Back Your Life* and with whom I was sharing the booth. She suggested I talk to the Dometic people (the brand of my refrigerator) who had a booth at the rally. I went looking for them. I explained my problem and was told that a repairman was on the grounds.

"Any ideas of what it could be?" I asked. "It's only a year old."

"Could be anything. They'll have to test all the circuits. Call the repairman," he said and I was dismissed with a look that said "beat it, lady."

As I walked back to the camper I ran into Judy and Roger Hellewege, a couple I had met at the Wyoming State Rally just a couple of weeks before.

"We were just coming to see you," said Judy.

I went into a brief description of my refrigerator problem and Judy asked if I was in dry dock.

"Yes," I replied.

"Your battery is running low," she said. "Run your generator if you have one."

I returned to the camper and turned on the generator. The light went from "check" to "AC" immediately. It has been working perfectly ever since.

I told my neighbor about it and he said that is exactly what he would have recommended. I told some of the members of the singles' group and they all concurred.

It seems that the only two who didn't know how to solve the problem were the people from the Dometic Company and me. Except now I know.....maybe someone should tell Dometic.

Port Aransas

I don't know what I expected when I drove my camper onto the ferry in Aransas Pass for the blink-of-an-eye-and-it's-over ride to Port Aransas. I drove off following a big red truck with a fifth-wheel hitch in the bed, the driver having offered to be my guide to Island Resort RV Park. Two minutes later I was standing in the parking lot waving a thank you to my pathfinder.

It didn't take long to fall in love with the place. Port A, as it is called by the locals and winter Texans alike, is one of the few places since my European camping days where I am right in the heart of town. I love not having to leave a trail of bread crumbs or empty wine bottles to find my way out of some wooded or off-the-beaten-track retreat that most North American campers seem to prefer

On my first day out, I hopped onto the free trolley that stopped right in front of the campground. It proceeded out to the bird sanctuary, for which Port Aransas is famous, before returning to the campground and then out and about the town. I was let out at the Computer Center and told that I would be picked up in exactly one hour.

The town does have a library with two computers available, but the Computer Center has thirty computers and although they are free of charge, the donation box sits right in front of the sign-in sheet so you can't miss it. After checking my e-mail I went outside to wait for the trolley.

It was a ten-minute wait in the heat of the day. I wandered in circles, fidgeted and finally came to rest against a truck parked on the street. I was surprised when the shopkeeper from the fish and tackle shop came out and asked if I was okay. "Would you like to wait inside, out of the sun?" he asked.

Joei Carlton Hossack

I thanked him profusely and told him I was waiting for the trolley. "I'd rather be ten minutes early than ten-seconds late," I responded and we both laughed.

When the trolley arrived, I hopped on, took a seat, toured all the beaches, had a birds-eye view of the main street and rode to the outskirts of town where the trolley driver took a five-minute break at Pioneer RV Park. I found the post office. The one thing I didn't get while riding the trolley was my bearings.

I discovered that everything I needed, when I chose to go directly from point A to point B, was within walking distance. From the campground it was about a mile and a bit to the Computer Center and the community center and about a mile to the J.E.L.M. Center, better known as the Winter Texas Center, and the Pollock Center. It was two long blocks to a reasonably well-stocked I.G.A. and two blocks, but in a different direction, to the library.

I was thrilled to find an active writers' group where everyone is welcome. A singles' group is just starting and I'm heading out there for the first time tonight after dinner. Every Friday night I'm out to the Pollock Center to listen to the guitars, banjos, an accordion, a piano and every other instrument that people bring along to a lively, sing-along jam session that is more often than not in tune. I'm booked into lecturing and book signing at four different places this month after being given lots of publicity in the local papers. Everyone seems to love the winter Texan.

I don't know what I was expecting when I drove off the ferry into Port Aransas but whatever it was, I got more.....much, much more.

Check your map. I'm sure you'll find this place easily enough. We are on Mustang Island, about twenty-five miles outside of Corpus Christi, Texas. Driving around, detailed map

Free Spirit

in hand, you'll never find it. IT IS ALWAYS FOGGED IN. Fortunately, a gentle little ninety-mile-an-hour breeze comes wafting in to blow the fog away.

Now where the heck did I drop those wine bottles!

Friends Along the Way

The sound of the telephone interrupting the meeting would normally have caused a glare or two but the others just looked my way and chuckled when they heard the sound emitting from my jeans pocket. It was four-fifteen on Saturday the fourth of December and I had recently changed my Nokia phone, with its thirty different rings, from the William Tell Overture to Jingle Bells. How could one's nerves be jangled to the sound of Jingle Bells so close to Christmas? I tried discretely to leave the building.

Even outside the connection was a poor one. From the few words I heard I knew it was my friend Amy Prestup calling from somewhere in the hinterland. She couldn't hear me any better than I could hear her. Through the intermittent static I heard her say "I'll call you back farther down the road." We both hung up.

Five hours later she called back. They were on a highway in Louisiana when they suddenly got a strong phone signal and pulled off to call me. "How's that," she said clear and crisp in my ear.

"Perfect," I responded. "Where are you?"

"Have no idea," she replied. "We're someplace in Louisiana. Do you want to meet us tomorrow at a KOA just past Lafayette? It's right off Highway 10. You can't miss it."

"Yes," I responded. "I'm leaving tomorrow morning and I'll be there as soon as I can. Can't wait to see you," I said excitedly.

I reminisced as I drove the two hundred and ninety-eight miles from Summerdale, Alabama to Lafayette, Louisiana. We had all been campers a long time. We had met in a city

Free Spirit

campground sometime in 1990. I don't remember the date. They had a sign in their motorhome window that said "English Books to Trade" and it was music to my ears hearing English spoken as we were used to. Amy and Norman were from New Jersey and Paul and I had met them one bus ride out of Rome, Italy.

We visited Rome together. We drove down the Amalfi Coast following each other. We toured Pompeii, Paestum and Ravello together. They drove to Sicily. We drove to Brindisi, Italy taking the ferry to Corfu, one of the Greek Islands. We met up, as planned, outside Athens. We celebrated Christmas in Gythion in the Peloponnese and New Year's on the Island of Crete. When the Gulf War broke out they preferred to remain on Crete and we sailed back to the mainland. We eventually all returned to America safely and remained friends through the years.....and now I would be camping with them side-by-side not in some distant land but at a KOA in Lafayette, Louisiana.

I pulled into the campground around three in the afternoon and as I drove the perimeter, I spotted their Safari Trek motorhome with their Tracker in tow in the second row. While checking in, I discovered that they had arranged for me to have the spot next to theirs. I paid. As I pulled in, Amy and Norman were standing outside waiting for a hug. I plugged in my electricity, turned on my refrigerator, gave them the five-cent tour of my truck camper and went into their motorhome for hours and hours and hours of yakking. It was like old times.

Through the snacks we talked about old times. Through the wine we talked about my solo life on the road. Through dinner we talked about where we were headed. Through dessert we talked about family and friends and after all was said and done they brought out pictures of their most recent trip.

They had celebrated Amy's fiftieth birthday and their twenty-fifth wedding anniversary on a guided tour through

Joei Carlton Hossack

Bhutan and Cambodia. Me…..envious…..no! Green is my natural color!

I don't know what time the evening ended. I just know it was late.

We had coffee and toast together the next morning. They headed out to Tucson, Arizona and I headed to Livingston, Texas.

Life at the Flying J

Shower number 520 is now ready.
Shower number 520 is now ready.

After a three hundred and twenty-five mile drive, much of it in gusty winds that blew me all over the road and without the hint of a campground for miles, I was delighted to see the sign that said seventeen miles to the Flying J. I didn't even mind having to drive two miles past Highway 39 north to Wisconsin, the road I planned on taking the following morning.

When I pulled into one of the many vacant spots, there were two other recreational vehicles already in place. One was a converted bus with "Nighty Nite" in big, block letters tattooed across the back and the other a large fifth-wheel with Washington license plates.

After walking around the store, checking the dinner menu, inspecting the buffet and seeing who was in the television lounge, I went back outside. I met Stephen, driver and head of the singing/comedy team making their home in the big beige-on-brown "Nighty Nite". He was heading for the garbage bin with a bursting-at-the-seams Wal-Mart bag. There were four in the bus, he explained, and they had several days to kill before their next gig in Pennsylvania.

I pointed out my rig and he had to comment on my Florida plates. "I hate working in Florida," he said. "The place is too old. I pulled into a Flying J down there and this real old guy lays down behind my motorhome and wouldn't move. I think he wanted me to run over him and put him out of his misery."

"How old was this old guy?" I asked. "Why was he allowed to run around loose if he was a menace?"

Joei Carlton Hossack

"The guy must have been fifty or more," Stephen answered fingering a well-trimmed beard that showed a few strands of gray.

"Huh, that old," I said. "Didn't know people lived that long," feeling I had to say something since I just had my fifty-eighth birthday.

We exchanged a few more Florida stories, some laughs and our business cards before he left to get rid of the bag in his hand and I returned to my camper.

The weather was the best it had been all day. The wind had died down and the sun was warm. A large motorhome pulling a car on a tow dolly with Iowa plates pulled in beside me. The right wheel on the dolly was askew. It seems that just as he pulled into the spot the axle broke.

"How lucky was that?" I asked. "Had you driven one more mile you would have been stranded on the highway. Would have been a hell of a place to spend the night."

While he off-loaded his car and jacked up the dolly I took out my deck chair and watched the show. He seemed to know exactly what he was doing and had the tools to do it with. The show was over when he left it all to head indoors. It was getting dark and cooling down to the point that I needed a sweatshirt.

I don't know when he finished the job and took off but he was gone long before I was up in the morning.

Shower number 561 is now ready.

Shower number 561 is now ready.

Not wanting to mess around in my kitchen, I decided on the buffet for dinner that night and was sorry with my choice. Everything managed to taste the same except, of course, my ice-cream dessert.

Free Spirit

Loitering outside their trailer were Diane and Mack from Quebec. We were just getting an interesting conversation going when a burgundy Buick pulled up beside us.

"Where are you folks from?" asked the passenger, a woman in her seventies or possibly older.

Diane said she was from Quebec while I confessed to having Florida plates but I lived wherever I parked my rig.

"Have you been to the Hegelar Carus Mansion?" she asked. "It's only about four or five blocks down the road."

We both admitted that we had never even heard of it since we were just passing through La Salle, Illinois.

"Hop in," she said, "and we'll take a run over there." She introduced herself as Sarah and her husband as Ed. She conducted the tour while he, the perfect chauffeur, drove slowly as she pointed out a bakery, a shoe repair and a few other stores that she frequented.

Well, the four or five blocks turned into four or five miles but they didn't seem to mind and we decided that it was well worth the trip. The place was closed and surrounded by a wrought-iron fence but we had an extraordinary view of the magnificent horseshoe staircase and porch at the formal entrance. We could also see some of the ceiling on the second floor since the lights shone brilliantly. Our hosts pointed out the zinc plant directly across the street from the mansion but it held little interest for any of us.

On the way back to the Flying J, our guide pointed out the road that led to the Wal-Mart and a large grocery store and a little farther down, the road that led to the post office.

Shower number 586 is now ready.

Shower number 586 is now ready.

I packed it in early since I had driven through a time change and although the clock read ten thirty-five my body said it was eleven thirty-five.

Joei Carlton Hossack

Shower number 721 is now ready.
Shower number 721 is now ready.
Damn, what time is it?..........four twenty-three the clock blinked steadily at me.
The rain started early, while it was still dark. By the time it was light it was pouring. I picked up a cup of coffee and decided to wait out the rain. "Nighty Nite" was still there. My friends from Quebec were still there. A few others had left.
Since Diane and Mack were heading for Alaska and I no longer needed my 2001 Milepost (the Alaskan bible), I bundled it up in a Wal-Mart bag and knocked on their door.
The morning of tea turned into an afternoon of dominoes and cards while the parking lot flooded with over two and a half inches of rain. When we couldn't sit anymore, we put on rain jackets and went into the store to check the television for the weather forecast. The rain was going to stick around another day.
Around four-thirty the rain stopped for a few minutes. Mack decided to make a run for it. He felt he could get in about three solid hours of daylight driving. We said good-bye in the store. They weren't even out of the parking lot when the heavens opened and dumped.
I wandered into the television room for truckers only. Within minutes I was talking to Barb, a twenty-five year veteran, who was sharing the driving with her father. Since they were hauling an extra-wide load they had to be off the road for the weekend. She explained some of the other rules of the trucker's life.
"I just filled up and instead of a discount on fuel they give us shower coupons. We have six extra coupons. Would you like to take a shower?" she asked after I explained that I lived in the really small motorhome and had been stuck at the Flying J a day longer than I expected.

Free Spirit

I gratefully accepted and went back to my rig to pick up my towel, soap and shampoo. So life goes at the Flying J.
Shower number 803 is now ready.
Shower number 803 is now ready.
Got to go. That one is mine.

Chian Singles Group

Although it was two years ago, I remember the first time like it was yesterday. I pulled into the campground in Douglas, Wyoming because I had a couple of weeks to kill before the first Great North American RV Rally in Gillette and liked the charged atmosphere of lots of people around. The Wyoming State Samboree, with over four hundred rigs, was just starting in Douglas and before they assigned me a spot, I was "accosted" while still in my vehicle by a tall, overly-friendly member of the "dreaded" singles' group.

I cringed and cowered like a caged animal and backed up into my seat as far as I could against the onslaught as she sang the praises of my singleness.

"If you're alone in there, you're just the person we want," she bellowed to the world in general and me in particular.

I wanted to run.....but where? I DON'T DO THE SINGLES' THING, the words screamed in my head. My instinct for self-preservation caused me to back away from my open side window. I had to force myself not to make the sign of the cross with the index fingers of both hands in my feeble attempt to ward off the devil in a blue jeans skirt and cowboy boots. Like a demented child, I turned beet red and babbled 'Yea! Okay! Whatever and see you later!'

I was relieved when a guy in a golf cart finally escorted me to my camping site. I was confident that I could hide from the clutches of the singles' group for most of the rally.

I took a couple of minutes to settle into my spot, connecting my water and electric. I grabbed my checkbook and

Free Spirit

high-tailed it back to the booth to register. Before I could finish writing the check, "Miss Congeniality" was on me like a vampire at a midnight virgin buffet.

I was barely able to finish the paperwork when I was whisked off to meet the gang. There were about twelve.....ten lecherous-looking women and two much older, delighted-to-be-surrounded-by-so-many-women, men.

I was invited to lunches, potlucks, four o'clock social hour with wine and nibblies and, of course, dinners out. We sat together during the evening entertainment and before long I was laughing and talking and telling dirty jokes as loud as they were. I was doing "the wave" with the group at the appropriate times and enjoying every minute of my time. At one of the social hours I did a travel lecture about my life on the road and was admired by everyone for my bravery.

Now where have the last two years gone? I have circled the United States a couple of times and driven through the center. I have lectured in a dozen or more States and Provinces. I have written two more books, have become a columnist for a few newspapers, have been the subject of several articles for local newspapers and national magazines and here I am, once again, at the Wyoming State Samboree.

I was sure I could sneak in unnoticed. Man-oh-man was I wrong! One member of the group had recognized my vehicle even before they spotted me. I was still unloading when the Chian Singles' Group, en masse, approached. I got the most heart-warming hugs from all my friends. It was followed by an invitation to the four-thirty social hour and a potluck dinner.

I was told that their motto is "turn off your engine and grab your fork" but they missed one key ingredient. Their motto should be:

Turn off your engine.
Hug a friend and invite him/her to dinner.

Joei Carlton Hossack

Grab a fork.
Thank you Chian Singles' for the warmest welcome in the country.

ABOUT THE AUTHOR:

Joei Carlton Hossack was born in February 1944 and raised in Montreal, Quebec, Canada. She has lived in Toronto, Canada, Los Angeles, California and Sarasota, Florida. She has spent most of the past thirteen years traveling the world gathering stories.

She is the author of Restless From The Start currently out of print and replaced by Free Spirit, Everyone's Dream Everyone's Nightmare, Kiss This Florida, I'm Outta Here, A Million Miles from Home and Alaska Bound and Gagged.

She is currently a solo, full-time RVer and travels the United States and Canada writing, lecturing and entertaining.

Joei Carlton Hossack can be reached at: JoeiCarlton@Hotmail.com